浙江工商大学外国语学院英语语言文学重点学科资助出版

破冰之旅——中国高校英语课堂的二语交流意愿个案分析

张露茜 著

To Break the Ice: Willingness to Communicate in L2 in English Lessons

Written by Luxi Zhang

浙江工商大学出版社
ZHEJIANG GONGSHANG UNIVERSITY PRESS

图书在版编目（CIP）数据

破冰之旅：中国高校英语课堂的二语交流意愿个案分析 / 张露茜著. —杭州：浙江工商大学出版社，2016.12

ISBN 978-7-5178-1477-1

Ⅰ. ①破… Ⅱ. ①张… Ⅲ. ①英语－课堂教学－教学研究－高等学校 Ⅳ. ①H319.3

中国版本图书馆 CIP 数据核字（2015）第 308229 号

破冰之旅——中国高校英语课堂的二语交流意愿个案分析

张露茜 著

责任编辑	黄静芬	
封面设计	林朦朦	
责任印制	包建辉	
出版发行	浙江工商大学出版社	
	（杭州市教工路 198 号　邮政编码 310012）	
	（E-mail：zjgsupress@163.com）	
	（网址：http://www.zjgsupress.com）	
	电话：0571－88904970，88831806（传真）	
排　　版	杭州朝曦图文设计有限公司	
印　　刷	杭州五象印务有限公司	
开　　本	880mm×1230mm　1/32	
印　　张	9.375	
字　　数	250 千	
版印次	2016 年 12 月第 1 版　2016 年 12 月第 1 次印刷	
书　　号	ISBN 978-7-5178-1477-1	
定　　价	32.00 元	

作者简介

　　张露茜,女,1983 年生,浙江瑞安人,现居杭州。浙江工商大学外国语学院英语专业讲师,博士。2005 年获浙江师范大学英语专业学士学位,2006 年获英国巴斯大学教育(英语语言教学)硕士学位,2012 年获香港教育学院①英语语言教育博士学位。主要讲授"基础英语""英语阅读""高级英语视听说"等课程。研究方向为英语教育、教育测量和话语分析。已在国内外学术期刊上发表论文十余篇,如在国外书籍出版社 Springer、国外高质量期刊 *Higher Education Quarterly* 与 *Educational Studies* 等上都曾发表论文。曾获研究生发表奖、优秀目标导师、优秀班主任、教学优胜奖等。多次参加国际会议。现主持和参与多项课题。

---

　　①　香港教育学院已于 2016 年正式更名为"香港教育大学"。

内容简介

在全球化影响下,中国社会对英语教学投注了大量心力。过往研究曾发现,具有高交流意愿者能在二语学习中获得较好成绩。但是教学实践反映出的问题是,英语专业的很多学生似乎在英语课堂上对参加口语活动的积极性并不高。因此,本书的研究目的为,发现阻碍与支持中国英语专业学生课堂交流意愿的个人与语境因素。四个研究问题分别为:1. 哪些个人因素阻碍或支持英语专业学生课堂交流意愿? 2. 哪些语境因素阻碍或支持英语专业学生课堂交流意愿? 3. 所有影响因素是如何互动以影响英语专业学生英语课堂交流意愿的? 4. 哪些教学改革能促进英语专业学生在英语课堂中的交流意愿?

本书通过在个案中混合不同的研究方法,期望获得对复杂的教学环境与过程的丰富理解。研究一为发现学生的个人因素,使用了问卷调查的方式;研究二为调查语境因素,先进行教学资料的审阅分析,再到课堂观察,最后是教师采访;研究三为进一步挖掘学生对当前课堂语境因素的回馈,通过学生的叙事、刺激回想、半建构式访谈取得。研究意义即,为英语专业学生提供最大化交流意愿的教学建议。研究发现,高英语口语水平与低焦虑能促进英语专业学生的交流意愿。但是,Wen 与 Clément(2003)的中国学生课堂交流意愿概念模型中的其他因素阻碍英语专业学生的交流意愿。三个研究的发现最终构建成一个修改后的中国英语学习者课堂交流意愿金字塔模型。

Statement of Originality

I, Luxi, Zhang, hereby declare that I am the sole author of the book and the material presented in this book is my original work except those indicated in the acknowledgement. I further declare that I have followed the policies and regulations on academic honesty.

Luxi, Zhang

November, 2016

Abstract

Under the influence of globalization in China, enormous attention is being paid to English learning and teaching. Previous research suggests that higher willingness to communicate (WTC) can lead to better achievement in learning a second language. However, it seems that many Bachelor of English (BE) students in Chinese universities are not likely to be actively involved in speaking activities in their English classes. Thus, the purpose of this research is to investigate what personal and contextual factors hinder or assist BE students' WTC in English language classrooms in China. Four research questions are posed: (1) What personal factors hinder or enable individual BE students' spoken English in English classrooms? (2) What contextual factors hinder or assist the students' spoken English in English language classrooms? (3) How do these factors interact to influence WTC in English language classrooms? (4) What pedagogical changes can enhance BE students' WTC in English classrooms?

By mixing methods within a single site case study, it was expected that a rich understanding of the complexities of the pedagogical environment and process could be obtained. Questionnaires were used to survey student personal factors, then inspection of teaching documents and classroom observations, followed by teacher interviews, were used to study the contextual factors of learning. Student narratives, stimulated recalls and semi-structured interviews were used to further elucidate student responses to contextual factors. The goal was to suggest pedagogical strategies that would maximize WTC in English language classrooms for all BE students in the case study site. It was found that both peaking English proficiency and low anxiety facilitated BE students' WTC. But other factors in Wen and Clément's (2003) Chinese WTC model hindered students' WTC. Finding of three studies suggested a modified three-dimensional Chinese L2 WTC pyramid model.

Keywords: WTC, Chinese culture, BE students, English language classrooms

Acknowledgements

I would not have completed this book without the guidance and support of many people. First, I am heartily thankful to my principal supervisor, Professor Bob Adamson, whose supervision, encouragement and support from the preliminary to the concluding level enabled me to develop an understanding of the subject.

I then wish to express my sincere gratitude to my associate supervisor, Associate Professor Dr. Elizabeth Walker for her expert advice.

I also owe my deepest gratitude to Associate Professor Gavin Brown in Auckland University, New Zealand. While he was teaching at the Hong Kong Institute of Education[1], I had learned a great deal about the quantitative research methods from him and he also co-supervised my thesis at the proposal stage. I would like to thank him for his later support and comments to the quantitative data analysis of the thesis.

Many thanks to the internal and external examiners; they spent their valuable time evaluating my thesis and provided useful comments.

---

[1] The Hong Kong Institute of Education was entitled as The Education University of Hong Kong in 2016.

My grateful thanks go to both teachers and students in the case study site, for their support and cooperation to my research.

Great appreciation goes to my classmates and friends at the institute for sharing ideas and invaluable discussions. I also would like to thank staff in the graduate school for helpful faculty support to meet my thesis timeline.

Last but not least, I would like to thank my family, my parents, sister Jane and husband, for their love and unconditional support.

Preface
Bob Adamson

Chair Professor of Curriculum Reform; Head, Department of
International Education & Lifelong Learning; Director,
Centre for Lifelong Learning Research & Development,
The Education University of Hong Kong

Speaking English is a challenge for many non-native speakers.
The language has many awkward sounds, such as consonant clusters,
to twist the tongue, and tricky stress and intonation patterns that
convey different meanings.

Many English learning programmes in China offer courses in
phonetics to assist students. Mastering the skills of producing
spoken language takes time and effort. A few years ago, I found
some wonderful textbooks produced by the People's Education
Press for junior secondary school students in the early 1960s.
Each passage in the textbooks that were published in 1961 had
stress and intonation marks to help the students, while the
syllabus (People's Education Press, 1963, in translation) for the
next series of textbooks set out these aims in relation to
speaking:

Junior Secondary Year 1
 • Mastering the accurate pronunciation of single and double

syllabus words that conform to regular pronunciation patterns; reading all lessons aloud and reciting the passages

• Speaking by imitating passages and using conventional conversation; understanding simple classroom language

• Acquiring about *600* words and a few idioms

Junior Secondary Year 2

• Reading aloud clearly and correctly; mastering stress and intonation of simple sentences; being able to recite about 80% of passages

• Asking and answering questions relating to the passages; understanding and responding to classroom language

• Acquiring another 600 words or so and a few idioms

Junior Secondary Year 3

• Reading the passages fluently with correct pronunciation and intonation; being able to recite about 70% of passages

• Answering questions relating to the passages; talking about familiar daily life topics; understanding the teacher's introduction to the passage; participating in conversations with the teacher about certain classroom activities

• Acquiring another 600 words or so and a few phrases

I cite these examples at length in order to demonstrate the enormous difficulties inherent in learning spoken English in China, particularly at a time when contact with foreigners was limited and technology was far less advanced than it is today. It took three years of study for students to become familiar with the phonetics and suprasegmental patterns of English, and to acquire the ability to conduct simple, everyday conversations. Nowadays, the available technology and the opportunities for speaking English may have improved, but the personal challenges of producing English sounds have not become smaller.

The challenges are not limited to sound production. Like Chinese, the English language is also rich in culture, which is a double-edged sword for learners. The richness undoubtedly contributes to the beauty of the language, but the cultural content can be obscure. Some metaphors can puzzle learners in China. What does "You're batting on a sticky wicket" mean? (This was feedback from a lecturer at a UK university to a foreign student. It actually means that the argument in the student's essay was not very solid, but the student—who was unfamiliar with the game of cricket—found it very hard to understand.) Not surprisingly, learners of English hesitate to speak in public. It takes courage.

On my frequent visits to China, I am always impressed by the courageous people who talk to me in English. I find them in many walks of life—very young and very old, white-collar and blue-collar, urban and rural. English corners in public squares and parks are amazing phenomena, as people hold animated discussions about an array of subjects. Yet I am told by many people that English standards in China are very low and the teachers of English are poor in quality. I disagree. Standards are extremely high, considering the linguistic environment, and teachers are extremely good, considering the other demands on students' learning.

Nevertheless, speaking out is definitely a challenge in a society that values face, harmony and self-effacement.

3

Classrooms, in particular, are highly pressured environments, and many teachers have remarked that their students seem to be "struck dumb" in English lessons. It is an area of student learning that has not been well understood in the past, but now Luxi's research enlightens us. This excellent book investigates the willingness of Chinese students to communicate in English and pinpoints the reasons that facilitate or hinder the process. Armed with the important insights contained in this book, teachers and students will be able to work together so this generation and future generations of learners can overcome the challenges in becoming effective English speakers.

Reference

People's Education Press (1963). *Yingyu Jiaoxue Dagang* (*English Syllabus*). Beijing: People's Education Press.

Table of Contents

List of Tables

List of Figures

Chapter 1
Introduction

1.1 Research problem

At present, English plays a vital role as an international language for developing the socio-economy, politics and education domains (Graddol, 2006; Kirkpatrick, 2007). That means currently English language learning is of great importance even to non-native English speakers. Thus, there are more and more speakers of English around the world for the purpose of communication, socio-economic development and academic exchanges. In China, enormous attention is being paid to English language learning. For instance, Xu (2002) estimates more than ninety percent of college and university students are taking compulsory English courses in China. In 2011, there were 2,429 colleges and universities in China, including 820 national universities for four-year undergraduate students, 1,228 national three-year higher vocational colleges, 311 independent institutions and 70 national validated campus schools (*China Education Newspaper*, 2011).

Since 1993, English language curriculum in China has been integrated with globalization trends for "developing trade, culture and scientific knowledge" (Adamson, 2004, p. 198). However, Chinese learners of English are well known for their "silent English". "Silent English" in China is "a metaphor showing an English learner is unable or cannot fluently speak out what one has learned, or rather speak influent Chinglish" (Zhao, 2009, p. 154). Chinglish is the way of speaking "in Mandarin sprinkled with English words and phrases or in English with a Mandarin-induced syntax" (Qing & Wolff, 2003, p. 30). A traditional Chinese philosophy, namely Confucianism, as Hu (2002) suggested, may be one major factor in how Chinese students learn to communicate "silently" in a second language. Under the influence of Confucianism, the way of English education in China is mostly exam-orientated and oral English is often neglected by teachers in China, leading to silent English among learners of English (Huang & Pan, 2011). Two aspects of Chinese cultural values seem to contribute to learners' unwillingness to communicate inside English language classrooms; that is, "other-directed self (face-protected orientation and the insider effect) and the submissive way of learning" (Wen & Clément, 2003, p. 19).

Thus, many university students who are studying Bachelor of English (BE) programmes may not be very willing to speak English in their English language classrooms. BE students are chosen in this study, as a new aim of cultivating inter-disciplinary BE students rather than single English language subject talents was established with the permission from the Ministry of Education under the market economy needs in China (ELT Advisory Board under the Ministry of Education, 2000). Since my research interest is on the study of BE students' spoken English learning, it may be informative to examine what happened to BE students after the educational reform in 2000.

1.2 Research motive

In second language (L2) learning, willingness to communicate (WTC) is a learner's "readiness to enter into discourse at a particular time with a specific person or persons, using a L2" (MacIntyre et al. , 1998, p. 547) both in and outside classrooms. Moreover, MacIntyre et al. noted that WTC is the primary goal in second language teaching and learning. As a teacher of English in a Chinese university, I perceived that active BE students inside classrooms tended to be among the academically better performing students. They may be more confident in their spoken English and more willing to contribute to classroom activities. However, a great many other BE students usually relate their desire to learn English well to patiently listening to the teacher, taking notes and memorizing in English classrooms. In order to develop students' communicative competence in spoken English, how teachers can construct supportive classroom context and help students learn from high WTC students is an issue we consider. This research is therefore used to solve the puzzle.

Meanwhile, recently, a number of L2 WTC studies have been conducted in different countries with different cultural orientations both in and outside classrooms and the importance of possessing WTC in second language learning has been demonstrated cross-culturally (e. g. Cao & Philp, 2006; Centinkaya, 2005; de Saint Léger & Storch, 2009; Kang, 2005;

MacIntyre & Doucette, 2010; Wen & Clément, 2003). There is a need to investigate the factors contributing to low WTC BE students and develop possible solutions that turn such students into high WTC students. Such understanding would improve students' spoken English proficiency in English language classrooms in China and contribute to China's international objectives. Facing BE students' unwillingness to communicate in classrooms problem, the research aims to find out what personal and contextual factors hinder or enable BE students' WTC in spoken English in English language classrooms in China.

1.3 Research aim and questions

The purpose of this study is to investigate the personal and contextual factors influencing WTC in spoken English in English language classrooms in China. The research questions are as follows:

Q1: What personal factors hinder or enable individual BE students' spoken English in classrooms?

Q2: What contextual factors hinder or assist BE students' spoken English in English language classrooms?

Q3: How do these factors interact to influence WTC in spoken English in English language classrooms?

Q4: What pedagogical changes can be drawn to enhance BE students' WTC in English classrooms?

It is intended that questionnaires will answer Research Questions 1, 3 and 4 related to the personal factors that influence BE students' WTC in speaking in English language lessons in China. Qualitative methods such as documents, observations and semi-structured interviews with teachers are combined to address Questions 2 to 4 related to contextual factors that influence BE students' WTC. Then, student narratives, stimulated recalls and semi-structured interviews with students are used to answer Questions 1, 3 and 4 related to personal factors. Answers obtained from the two sets of data (quantitative and qualitative data) are later integrated to reveal the research aim in depth.

1.4 Significance of the study

Table 1

Categories of students' WTC according to classroom contextual factors

WTC of students	Classroom contextual factors	
	Weak, not supportive	Strong, supportive
High WTC	1. Capable, willing but traditional context does not require WTC	2. Capable, willing and progressive context requires and helps increase WTC
Low WTC	3. Weak, unwilling and traditional context does not require WTC	4. Weak, unwilling but progressive context requires and helps increase WTC

The goal of this research is to answer research questions that may address the research problem of why many BE students are reluctant to communicate in spoken English inside English language classrooms. This is an important goal, as studies have shown that increased WTC can lead to better academic performance in second language learning (MacIntyre et al.,

1998). Through WTC investigation in spoken English with BE students, it is expected that this research will find out personal and contextual factors that hinder or facilitate students' WTC in spoken English. Speculation of study implications is based on Table 1, which shows four categories of students' WTC according to contextual factors.

The findings of this research may provide some enlightenment for teaching Chinese students English around the world, since it is likely that the cultural norms of Chinese university students may well affect Chinese students wherever they are.

1.5 Outline of this book

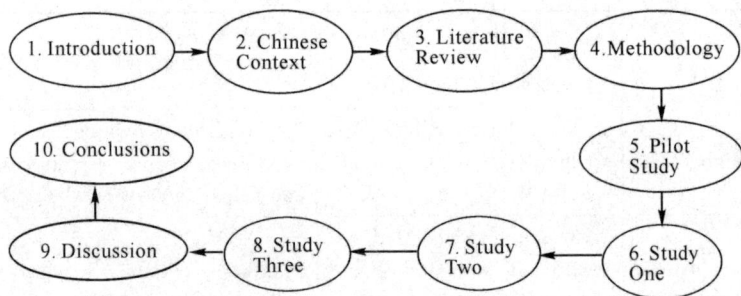

Figure 1. Flow of the book.

Figure 1 outlines the book. The following two chapters first review the Chinese context regarding English in China, college English and WTC in L2; and then focus on the development of WTC literatures and studies in the first and second language fields. Wen and Clément (2003) designed a Chinese model of L2 WTC in classrooms, which is fundamental to this research. In their model, DC (desire to communicate with a specific person) is an indispensable part and differs from WTC. The Chinese conceptualization of L2 WTC model embeds influential factors from DC to WTC.

Chapter 4 shows the research design, the case study approach, research setting and participants, instruments, data analysis procedures and ethical issues. By mixing methods within a single site case study, it is expected that a rich understanding of the complexities of the pedagogical environment and process can be obtained. Studies in this book are divided into three phases for searching personal and contextual dimensions of WTC factors by mixing quantitative and qualitative methods. Then, pilot questionnaire outcomes are mentioned in Chapter 5.

The next three chapters describe the findings and discussion of the three studies concerning BE students' WTC in speaking in English classrooms. Chapter 6, that is, Study One, analyzes the quantitative CFA (confirmatory factor analysis) and SEM (structural equation modeling) findings at the personal level. Chapter 7, that is, Study Two, and Chapter 8, that is, Study Three, depict the thematically coded qualitative findings at the student personal and contextual levels. Key issues are discussed and the four research questions are answered. Chapter 9 discusses the findings of the three studies as a whole. In addition, the last chapter, Chapter 10, summarizes the whole book and pedagogical recommendations for enhancing BE students' WTC in speaking in English language classrooms. Also, limitations of the study are included.

Chapter 2
Chinese Context

This chapter will review the Chinese context, embedding English in China, College English and WTC for the purpose of covering some key ideas from research questions. First, it may be worth noting that English in China has a long cultural, political and linguistic history. In this case, the background information of English development in China can be provided. Second, China English is mentioned. Third, college English is reviewed since the project focuses on the study of BE students. Fourth, WTC is defined and the main theories drawn upon in the project are highlighted.

2. 1 *English in China*

The contact between British maritime traders and the southern Chinese (Guangzhou and Macau) was first recorded in 1637 (Bolton, 2003). In his book, Bolton shows a general map of English in China from the year 1637 to present. In contrast, Adamson (2002) presented a clear picture of the evolution of English in China since 1911. Before 1949, the main functions of English were for ideas and then for diplomacy and interaction. From 1949 to 1960, English was confined to mainly science and technology areas. Then, the first renaissance came with English posters in the school curriculum. From 1961 to 1966, English was used for modernization and international understanding purposes. During the "Great Cultural Revolution" in 1966— 1976, English speakers were regarded as suspect forces. There was a recovery in a slow speed during the following six years and English again became the language for modernization. Then from 1982 till now, there were strong demands of learning English in schools as well as in school curricula, resulted from economic development under the open-door policy. At present, English is nationally taught as a compulsory subject for students from junior secondary to senior high schools and also for most colleges and universities. In addition, English classes in upper primary school are provided in schools that have the capacities to offer them (Jin & Cortazzi, 2003).

Accordingly, over time, the role of English in China has changed from English as a foreign language (EFL) to English as an international language (EIL), then to what is more recent view of English as a Chinese language (ECL) (Edwards, 2007). The former two roles are based on the standard British or American English whereas the latter one builds on the variation within Chinese varieties. Moreover, for EIL, most Chinese learners are actually learning English for intranational and international communication purposes; for ECL, the communication can be between native speakers of a specific dialect, such as Cantonese and Putonghua. Edwards concludes, "Perhaps the most feasible and realistic model of English language teaching in China will one day be a Chinese language— China English. " (p. 278)

Aligned with the history of English in China, the English language curricula over time vary along with the changes of social and political climates in China. Adamson (2004) identifies five phases of the features of English language curriculum in China since 1949, namely, "the end of Soviet influence" "towards quality in education" "the 'Great Cultural Revolution'" "modernization under Deng Xiaoping", and "integrating with globalization" (p. 198). The content of the textbooks in the first four phases more or less contains some politicized texts, especially in the third phase. In contrast, the last phase embeds some cultural information instead of politicized texts. At the same time, the intended learning methods in the first four phases are "structural, grammar-translation and audiolingualism", whereas the last phase shifts to "eclectic: functional/notional-structural" ways of learning and since the year 2000 "task-based learning" is added in (p. 198). In China, the pedagogy for the first four phases expresses in the teacher-centered knowledge transmission of grammatical points to students with the main focus on developing reading and writing skills, while the last phase is a more communicative way for developing the four skills of listening, speaking, reading and writing skills under the teacher's guidance (and students' autonomy in task-based learning) (Adamson, 2004).

The global spread of English with its advantages and disadvantages, impacts current China in many areas. The political and economic developments stimulate the enthusiasm for learning English (Graddol, 2006). For instance, Shanghai prepared for its 2010 Expo by setting goals to improve its citizens' English language skills. However, the influence of

English is not limited in these two fields. Knowledge of English can bestow a sense of status to English learners (Kirkpatrick, 1999) and thus can be beneficial for young Chinese university graduates (Xu, 2002). For instance, some students may wish to extend their studies abroad in English language speaking countries while some others, such as some Bachelors of Business English students, may want to work in joint ventures.

Nonetheless, Ferguson (2006) put forward two main English-related inequalities for periphery countries like China, that is, "inequality in communication between native and non-native speakers of English, and socio-economic inequalities arising from differential access to English" (p. 144). To minimize the inequalities, he calls for a policy "involving both an enhanced role for local languages and democratization of access to English" and democratization here relates to "the enhancement of access to English for disadvantaged groups in circumstances where the language is necessary for mobility and participation yet relatively inaccessible" (p. 145).

Edwards (2007) mentioned that the teaching of English culture is unavoidable. Because not only language and culture are inseparable, but also the real teaching textbooks and situations in China involve direct and indirect English ways of communicative teaching. For example, group works require interactions between peers instead of direct knowledge transmission from the teacher to students. The circumstance is the same for Chinese BE students, as British and American English is regarded as the standard in English learning.

Given cultural imperialism attracts many authors' attentions in ELT field, the teaching of CLT (communicative language teaching) becomes a controversial issue. The analysis of culture imperialism is "the sum of process by which a society is brought into the modern world system and how its dominating stratum is attracted, pressured, forced, and sometimes bribed into shaping social institutions to correspond to, or even promote, the values and structures of the dominating center of the system" (Schiller, 1976, p. 9). For instance, English speaking countries' educational aid projects to non-English speaking countries can make those receiving countries to accept the cultural values of English speaking countries through the teaching of English (Phillipson, 1992).

CLT had been regarded as one means of cultural imperialism (MaKay, 2003). Nonetheless, McKay (2003) argued that it seems inappropriate to view CLT as the best method for English language teaching, as CLT is a "culturally-influenced methodology" (p. 17). Proponents of McKay's view claimed it is probably necessary for non-native learners of English "to identify themselves, and to be identified, as competent, authoritative users of their own variety as opposed to imperfect or deficient speakers of British or American standard English" (Ferguson, 2006, p. 146).

A current view of CLT is changed to include both communicative and non-communicative classroom activities (Richards, 2006; Savignon, 2005, 2007). To develop communicative competence is the central goal of CLT. But Richards (2006) further suggested CLT employs what can best facilitate learning. Savignon (2005) claimed that though group and pair work are helpful in many contexts to provide more chances and motivation for communication, they cannot be seen as equal to CLT. CLT also includes "metalinguistic awareness of knowledge of rules of syntax, discourse, and social appropriateness" (Savignon, 2007, p. 213). Meanwhile, if a task such as brainstorming can be best carried out through group works, this type of interaction in L2 teaching cannot be completely abandoned. In light of their perspectives, China English will be referred to in the next section.

2.1.1 Definitions of China English

The teaching of China English meets the need of developing communicative competence among Chinese students. Authors debate over the definitions of China English. The landmark definition of China English is "the English used by the Chinese people in China, being based on standard English and having Chinese characteristics" (Wang, 1994, p. 7). However, Li (1993) challenges the first two elements of Wang's definition. For one thing, China English is not confined to China. For another thing, he doubts if there is standard English in China; rather, he would like to use the term "Normative English" (p. 19). In this case, he defines China English as "the lexis, sentence structure and discourse that have Chinese characteristics. It takes Normative English as a core, and it expresses things that are uniquely Chinese. It bears no mother tongue (Chinese) interference, and it is involved in English communications by means of transliterations, loan translations and semantic shifts" (p. 19). However, Xie (1995) later argued that China English has Chinese interference. By 1997, Jia and Xiang (1997) regarded China English as a variety of English. Similarly, Wei and Fei (2003) identified China English as "an English with Chinese characteristics and culture—to be regarded

as a member of the family of English in its own right" (p. 44).
Regardless of the difference in their definitions, the perception of
Chinese characteristics is recognized by all of them. The Chinese
characteristics can be seen from the impacts of dialects and
Putonghua (Mandarin) on English.

2.1.2 *The impacts of dialects and Putonghua on English*

The Chinese characteristics of China English can be seen,
for instance, from the discussions on its phonology. Zhao and
Campbell (1995) suggest that China English has its "unique
features at the phonetic, lexical, syntactic, semantic, and
discourse level" (p. 377). Nevertheless, the extent of and the
reason for this uniqueness are not clearly stated by them. Kirkpatrick
and Xu (2002) pointed out that China English is varied with regard to
its phonology. The reason is "the varied pronunciation of Chinese
dialects and the resultant varied pronunciation of Putonghua...
strongly suggest that the pronunciation of China English will also
be varied" (p. 270). Besides, they describe a feature of China
English, that is, it has "syllable-over stress-timed rhythm"
(Edwards, 2007, p. 275). China English is affected by the
Chinese rhythm. The English rhythm is stress-timed and English
has different syllable length and weight whereas the Chinese
rhythm is syllable-timed with the same length and weight in all
syllables (Fan, Chen & Lin, 1998). Moreover, Chinese
students' English is affected by their dialects in terms of the
pronunciation and this may cause unintelligibility for
comprehension of their words to non-PRC teachers and
sometimes it may also be hard for people with different dialects
to understand each other's English (Ho, 2003).

There are a few studies on phonological differences of people from different regions in China (e. g. Ho, 2003; Deterding, 2006). To investigate the interference of dialects in English, Ho (2003) studied 39 students from different parts of China in the years 1996 and 1998 in CELE (the Centre for English Language Communication). The aim of the study is to unfold the problems for comfortable intelligibility rather than native-like pronunciation. The study shows that those students from central part of China such as Hubei, Henan and Shandong have more pronunciation problems than other students. Conversely, students from Beijing and coastal cities like Suzhou and Guangzhou are more fluent in spoken English and much better in pronunciation, attributable to more access to English programmes on TV and radios. Students from central China tend to substitute /n/ for /l/ whereas southern Chinese may mispronounce /v/ for /b/ (*activity* sounds like *actibity*) or /v/ for /w/ (*everywhere* sounds like *everyvhere*). However, the study displays that it is difficult for most students, especially those from southern China, to pronounce consonants /r/ and /l/ correctly in two-syllabic or polysyllabic words. The second most difficult sound is the fricative /θ/ and the third is the nasal /ŋ/. For the former, students tend to pronounce it as /s/ or /t/. For the latter, it may be substituted with /n/. More recently, recording the pronunciation of 13 students from north-east, east and central China, Deterding (2006) denoted that some features of their speech might be part of China English. Whilst each participant was required to read a passage and participate in a short interview, five major characteristics of their pronunciation emerged as: applying an added vowel preceding word-final plosives particularly when the following word is beginning with a consonant; avoiding reduced vowels particularly in function words; heavy nasalized vowels after a final nasal consonant; substituting /s/ for /θ/, /z/ for /d/ or /ð/, /x/ for /h/; and emphasizing sentence-final pronouns.

In addition to the phonological characteristics just mentioned, Kirkpatrick (2007) provides a list of other features of China English in terms of lexis, grammar, pragmatics and cultural conventions. The lexical features of China English include direct translation such as *four books*; nativized English words, such as *poker* into *pu-ke*; other culturally meaningful Chinese words in English, for example, *dragon*. *Four books* is called *si* (four) *shu* (book) in Chinese and they are the classical Confucius books. *Dragon* was the symbol of the emperor in ancient China and now it has positive benefits associated with fame, reputation and career. Furthermore, McArthur (2002) proposes that English is influenced by Chinese words in three groups: "food, health and medicine; behaviour and activities; objects and processes in the world" (pp. 357—358). For instance in food, *chopstick* is combined of the English word *stick* and the Pidgin English *chop*, which perhaps comes from the Cantonese *gap*, meaning quick or urgent. The grammar feature of China English, which is derived from Xu (2005), consists of a range of characteristics and many are parallel to the other varieties of English, for instance, subject pronoun copying. An example of subject pronoun copying is "some of my college classmates *they* like to dress up very much, and they don't like to study very much" (p. 315). Regarding the last feature of pragmatics and cultural conventions, Kirkpatrick (2007) uses Ha Jin's English fiction to express the Chinese cultural meaning of *guanxi*. Ha Jin is a novelist who comes from China and writes stories in English. *Guanxi* is the direct translation of relationship, but in the fiction it actually means making social networks with a figure that is important. Nimei in the fiction shows her hospitality to form network (*guanxi*) with Director Liao who in future can offer a better job for her husband Jiang Bing.

2. 2   *College English*

At the tertiary level, English (in China) began to be taught extensively in universities from the mid-1960s, especially in large cities (Gao, 2000). Since 1987, all students were required at least to pass the nation-wide College English Test (CET), Band 4. Though at present passing the CET 4 exam is no longer related to obtaining a bachelor's degree, the English certificate is valued in workplaces. Adamson (2004) suggested the present role of English in China is the highest in history. It is evidenced not only in setting up English as a vital subject in curriculum, but also in growing concerns of applying English as a MoI (medium of instruction) in many schools for the purpose of adopting bilingual education. Taking the university in this case study for example, all undergraduates have to study at least one compulsory English course and for Bachelor of English especially, their courses are carried out with English as a MoI.

Regarding teaching China English in China, Ferguson (2006) noted that the biggest hindrance on the way of English as a Lingua Franca (ELF) teaching models is " acceptability", resulting from " the persistence of the traditional notion that native-speaker-like competence is the ultimate benchmark of learning achievement" (p. 177). Edwards (2007) suggests that the variety of English needs to be taught in schools is China English. However, the English language teaching models in China are mostly NS (native-speaker)-based, especially the American English model (Hu, 2004, 2005; Jin, 2005). The L2 success of being native speakers in English is far out of reach for Chinese English learners, as few are going to meet this aim. Thus, "both teachers and students become frustrated by setting themselves what is in effect an impossible target" (Cook, 2002, p. 331). In this case, a strategy to enhance the legitimate status of English rests on raising the awareness of World Englishes (WE) (Jenkins, 2006).

Indicating the needlessness of learning NS-based English as well as reviewing some previous works in WE and ELF fields, Li (2007) ascertains the importance of promoting China English with regard to teachers, curricula and learner needs. First, most English learners in China study English from their English teachers who are second or foreign language learners of English. Local Chinese teachers understand learners' language as well as culture, which are not owned by native English teachers (Braine, 1999; Medgyes, 1994). Also, the local teachers' English is influenced by their mother tongue at different levels, which can be seen as a resource for English learners (Cook, 2002). Then, the culturally influenced curricula ought to suit learners' needs by involving Chinese culture rather than Anglo-American culture (Kirkpatrick, 2006; McKay, 2002, 2006). Xu (2002) cautioned that English teachers should select useful materials from existing textbooks as well as authentic language materials from a variety of sources for the sake of suiting students' level of English. Finally, the study of China English raises learners' confidence in English, enhances their English learning purposes and a sense of ownership is developed for the purpose of the communicative needs (Li, 2007).

2.3 *Willingness to communicate* (*WTC*)

In spite of the need to teach China English to develop communicative competence in English, many BE students in China are unwilling to speak in English classrooms. It is mentioned in Chapter 1 that L2 willingness to communicate (WTC) is a learner's "readiness to enter into discourse at a particular time with a specific person or persons, using an L2" (MacIntyre et al. , 1998, p. 547) both in and outside classrooms. The discourse in the WTC definition includes both spoken and written discourse (MacIntyre et al. , 1998). Many researchers have linguistically highlighted the important role of speech in language communication and acquisition (Halliday, 1990; Long, 1996; Swain, 1985, 1995, 2000). Long's (1996) Interaction Hypothesis suggested the essentiality of meaning negotiations of input to make the language comprehensive. However, Swain (1985, 1995, 2000) developed a Comprehensible Output Hypothesis and argued that L2 interactions might be more influenced by comprehensible output than input. Her studies of immersion students' L2 development found that students learnt to be native-like in listening and reading, but fell behind in writing and speaking. Thus, she suggested that learner output should be considered regarding written and oral proficiency and functional teaching of speaking such as increasing fluency (which implies automaticity) could develop oral proficiency. Moreover, Halliday (1990) compared speech and writing in language and suggested speech was a preparation for writing.

MacIntyre et al. also regard WTC as the primary goal in L2 learning. In this case, drawing on Bronfenbrenner's (1995) ecological perspective, under the influence of globalization and the macro-system of Chinese culture, WTC is placed at the center of the self and the systems while the micro-system of classroom is considered in the study (see Figure 2).

Wen and Clément (2003) presented a Chinese conceptualization of WTC in Figure 3. They suggested that Chinese students' WTC undergoes a complex process from desire to communicate with a specific person (DC) to general WTC. The development of WTC is influenced in their model by a variety of factors; such as, "societal context (group cohesiveness & teacher support), personality factors (risk-taking & tolerance of ambiguity), motivational orientations (affiliation & task-orientation) and affective perceptions (inhibited monitor & positive expectation of evaluation)" (Wen & Clément, 2003, p. 25). Since Chinese learners of English have the universal DC, the conceptualization implies Chinese learners of English have to conquer the four factors in order to achieve WTC. After reviewing the background of the book concerning the Chinese context, a detailed literature review of WTC can be presented in the next chapter.

WTC

Self

Micro system
(family, classroom, teachers&
peers)

Macro system: Chinese
culture

Globalisation

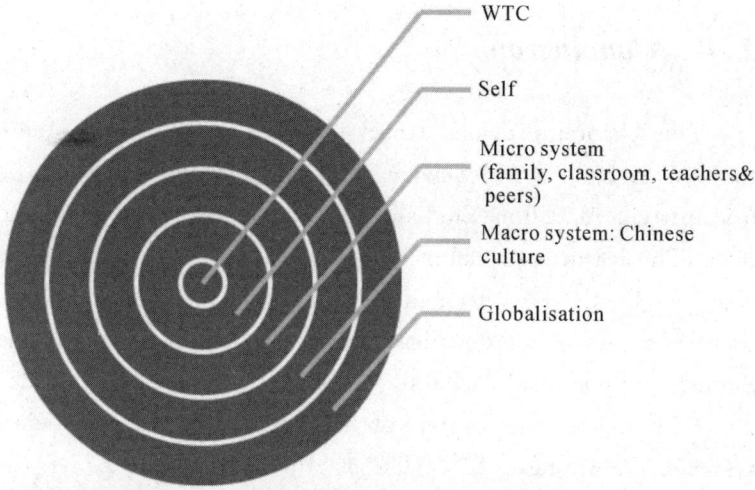

Figure 2. WTC in the micro- and macro-systems of developmental ecological systems (Bronfenbrenner, 1995).

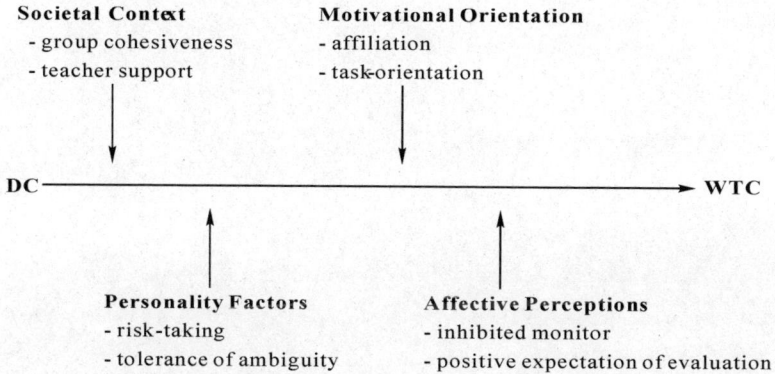

Societal Context
- group cohesiveness
- teacher support

Motivational Orientation
- affiliation
- task-orientation

DC ──────────────────────────────────► WTC

Personality Factors
- risk-taking
- tolerance of ambiguity

Affective Perceptions
- inhibited monitor
- positive expectation of evaluation

Figure 3. A Chinese conceptualization of WTC in classrooms (Wen & Clément, 2003).

2.4   Conclusion

This chapter provides a background review of the Chinese context. A historical review of the role of English in China is first introduced. China English as a variety of English is defined then. The features of China English are expressed in how it is impacted by Chinese dialects and Putonghua. Moreover, this chapter suggests that college English should accept China English for meeting teachers', curricula's and learners' needs. L2 WTC is in the center of the developmental ecological systems. A Chinese L2 WTC is then proposed to be the literature basis for this study.

Chapter 3
Literature Review

The purpose of this study is to explore what personal and contextual factors affect BE students' willingness to communicate in a university of China. In this chapter, relevant theories and studies are reviewed under three phases of establishment of WTC in L1, establishment of WTC in L2 and development of L2 WTC studies and theories outside and in China. Then, factors in the Chinese WTC model and a challenge for the model regarding the changed collectivism in China are depicted. The literature review of WTC theories can form the ground for later study discussions.

WTC feature: trait-like→trait-like &. contextual

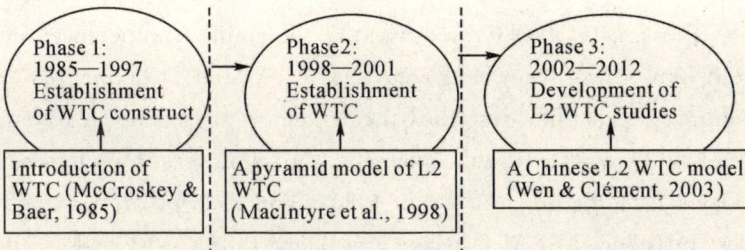

Phase 1: 1985—1997 Establishment of WTC construct	Phase 2: 1998—2001 Establishment of WTC	Phase 3: 2002—2012 Development of L2 WTC studies
Introduction of WTC (McCroskey & Baer, 1985)	A pyramid model of L2 WTC (MacIntyre et al., 1998)	A Chinese L2 WTC model (Wen & Clément, 2003)

WTC studies: Scales→+qualitative or mixed methods

Figure 4. WTC development from L1 to L2 since 1985.

Figure 4 shows three phases of WTC development since its introduction by McCroskey and Baer (1985). In the first phase from 1985 to 1997, WTC studies in L1 field found the causal relationships of personal factors such as motivation and attitudes to WTC. Built on L1 WTC findings, the second phase came with the emergence of a pyramid model of L2 WTC by MacIntyre et al. (1998). The feature of WTC changed from merely being trait-like to being trait-like and contextual. During 1998 to 2001, WTC studies were conducted in Canada based on the pyramid model to establish WTC construct in L2. In the third phase since 2002, more and more L2 WTC studies have been conducted in different countries across the world, applying not only scales, but also a variety of other qualitative or mixed qualitative and quantitative methods. During this time, a theoretical model of Chinese L2 WTC in English classrooms was developed by Wen and Clément (2003). The following sections will describe the three phases in detail.

3.1　Establishment of WTC in L1

Previously, WTC was treated as stable competence and trait-like (McCroskey & Baer, 1985). A trait is defined as "a summary term that describes the tendency to behave, feel, and think in ways that are consistent across different situations" (Davis & Palladino, 2004, p. 468). The concept of WTC was first introduced by McCroskey and Baer (1985). McCroskey and Richmond (1987) then regarded WTC as a personality construct. In first language learning field, the trait-like feature of WTC can be seen from its definition: "the one, overwhelming communication personality construct which permeates every facet of an individual's life and contributes significantly to the social, educational, and organizational achievements of the individual" (Richmond & Roach, 1992, p. 104).

McCroskey and Richmond (1989) emphasized the importance of WTC for learners. The more communication an individual learner has, the better evaluation from contexts such as schools can often be received. In contrary, having low willingness to communicate will reduce one's feeling of happiness in a society.

As the pioneer in building WTC theories, McCroskey's (1997) standpoint of trait-like WTC was developed from three sources: unwillingness to communicate (Burgoon, 1976), predispositions toward verbal behavior (Mortensen, Arntson & Lustig, 1977) and shyness (McCroskey et al. , 1981). Firstly, the unwillingness to communicate concept is about the avoidance of oral communication. Burgoon's (1976) self-reported unwillingness to communicate questionnaire includes two areas of approach—avoidance and reward. The former measures communication apprehension, while the latter examines the feeling of satisfaction within a group. It was found that unwillingness to communicate correlated only with the approach-avoidance aspect. Secondly, predispositions toward verbal behavior refer to that the amount of communication is consistent in different communication situations and a predisposition toward verbal behavior (PVB) scale was designed by Mortensen, Arntson and Lustig (1977). Thirdly, according to Leary (1983), shyness relates to social anxiety, which is made up of inner discomfort as well as outer anxious behaviors that a learner experienced in communication. Shyness is regarded as outer anxious behavior and shyness is defined as "the tendency to be timid, reserved, and most specifically, talk less" (McCroskey, 1997, p. 460). The designed McCroskey Shyness Scale (McCroskey et al., 1981) can be used to calculate the amount of talk and thus predict behavioral tendencies in communication.

Nevertheless, McCroskey (1997) criticized rather than presented a full picture of unwillingness to communicate predispositions; Burgoon's study only shows that towards communication the more fearful or anxious a person is, the less communication one tends to be involved in; Mortensen et al.'s predispositions toward verbal behavior just add the evidence that an individual's communication is regular to some extent; McCroskey Shyness Scale neglects the necessity of measuring on a personality basis.

McCroskey and Richmond (1990) suggest that communication apprehension (or to say, communication anxiety) and perceived communication competence are the two keys for forming WTC. In other words, a person can be willing to communicate when he or she is not anxious or apprehensive and feels competent to communicate with others. Their perspective was backed up by MacIntyre's (1994) study and a path model can be developed (see Figure 5). In order to investigate the WTC factors on a personality basis, MacIntyre used the unwillingness to communicate elements identified earlier by Burgoon (1976), which are communication apprehension, anomie, alienation, introversion, self-esteem and perceived communication competence. The results show that communication apprehension and perceived communication competence are the two strongly influential factors affected WTC. Willingness to communication affects frequency of communication; however, the hypothesis that there is direct influence of communication anxiety on perceived communication competence is not supported in the study.

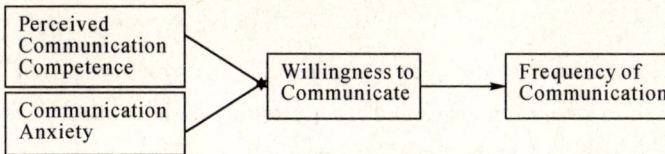

Figure 5. MacIntyre's (1994) willingness to communicate path model.

While developing WTC theories, a WTC scale was designed and then validated (McCroskey & Baer, 1985; McCroskey, 1992). The scale lists twenty situations for a person to indicate the percentage of times from zero of never to one hundred of always. Of the twenty situations, twelve items can be categorized in interactions with group discussion, meetings, interpersonal conversations and public speaking or grouped into communications with strangers, acquaintances and friends. The remaining eight are filter items for communicating with a specific person or persons, such as a secretary.

The WTC scale was applied in many studies in the first language field and there are some studies concerning cross-cultural issues. McCroskey and Richmond (1990) compared the study outcomes of Puerto Rican college students' WTC (McCroskey, Fayer & Richmond, 1985) with Australian, Micronesian, Swedish and USA students' WTC. Sallinen-Kuparinen, McCroskey and Richmond (1991) tested Finish students' WTC and then compared the findings with the students in the above two mentioned articles. These study results show that students' communication orientations differ significantly across different countries and cultures (Simic & Tanaka, 2008).

3.2　Establishment of WTC in L2

Gathering the study and theoretical outcomes in L1 WTC, the second phase emerges with a pyramid model of L2 WTC in 1998. Instead of viewing WTC as solely trait-like and stable in first language (L1) communication field, researchers concerned with the application of WTC in second language learning contexts have developed a heuristic model of both trait-like and contextual variables influencing WTC (MacIntyre et al. , 1998). Relating attitude and motivation theories, MacIntyre et al. (1998) argued that WTC in L2 communication is different from WTC in L1 communication in that WTC in L2 is also contextual. They perceive that despite the fact that some students with low competence in L2 may tend to be willing to communicate in a second language, some students with high language competence may be unwilling to communicate in that language. Many learners' WTC differs over time and be contextual.

While pointing out that L2 WTC is one primary goal in second language learning and teaching domains, they suggest a heuristic model of twelve variables influencing WTC (see Figure 6). The model has two constructs, that is, the first three layers are contextual whereas variables in layers Ⅳ, Ⅴ and Ⅵ are enduring and trait-like. The four contextual variables of L2 use, willingness to communicate, desire to communicate with a specific person and state communicative self-confidence vary in different contexts with different individuals and task topics. The six enduring variables of interpersonal motivation, intergroup motivation, L2 self-confidence, intergroup attitude, social context and communicative competence in layers Ⅳ (motivational propensities) and Ⅴ (affective-cognitive context) are quite similar to the points in Gardner's (1985) socio-psychological model. The last layer includes intergroup climate and personality, indicating one's communication with the society and the individual.

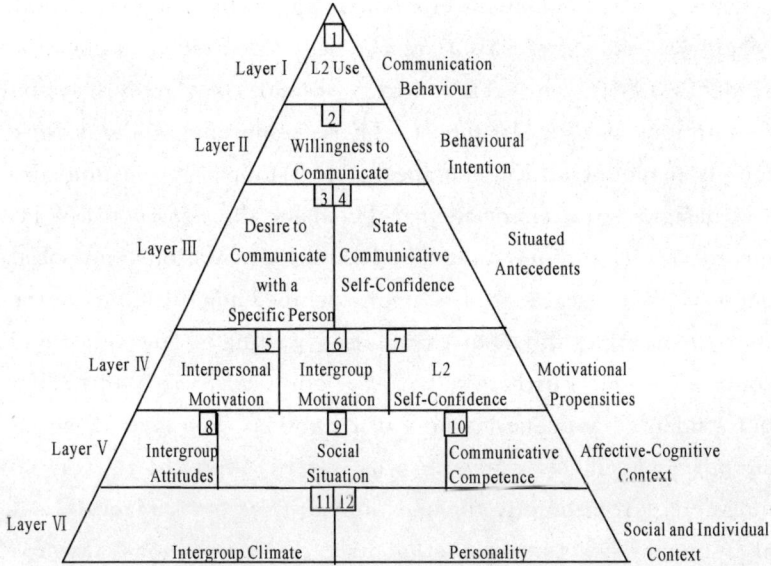

Figure 6. Heuristic model of variables influencing WTC (MacIntyre et al., 1998).

Reviewing previous literatures in WTC, Matsuoka and Evans (2005) analyzed the establishment of WTC constructs in

L1 and then in L2. For instance, they distinguished the importance of the six layers in MacIntyre et al. 's (1998) heuristic L2 WTC model. That is, in the WTC pyramid model (see Figure 6), the importance of the six layers reduces from the top to the bottom. As the bottom three layers are stable variables, the authors suggested that the level of WTC can be tested through the first three contextual layers.

Based on the pyramid WTC model (MacIntyre et al., 1998), L2 WTC scales inside and outside classrooms were developed by MacIntyre et al. 's (2001) study in Canada. Paying attention to individual differences in authentic communication, MacIntyre et al. (2001) researched L2 French immersion students' WTC in relation to second language learning orientations and social support. These grade nine students were mostly monolingual English speakers. A four-part questionnaire was designed to examine their WTC inside the classroom, WTC outside the classroom, language learning orientations and social support. WTC scales are five points, embedding questions in the four learning skills of reading, writing, speaking and comprehension. Furthermore, a six-point scale was used to find out students' language learning orientations. The level of social support gained by students was tested through yes or no questions. According to the questionnaire outcome, MacIntyre et al. summarised that the students' five orientations towards language learning of travel, job, friendship with Francophones, personal knowledge, and school achievement were positively correlated with WTC in the four skills both inside and outside classrooms. Social support especially from friends stimulated higher levels of WTC outside the classroom; however, the effect of social support was not influential in the classroom. The next section will review the third phase concerning the development of L2 WTC.

3. 3 Development of L2 WTC studies and theories

Since 2002, the evolution of WTC in the third phase has been moving towards the development of L2 WTC studies and theories. Grounded in MacIntyre et al. 's (1998) theories, L2 WTC has attracted many researchers' attention recently (Cao & Philp, 2006; de Saint Léger & Storch, 2009; Fushino, 2010; Kang, 2005; MacIntyre et al. , 2002; MacIntyre, Burns & Jessome, 2011; MacIntyre & Doucette, 2010; MacIntyre & Legatto, 2011, Matsubara, 2007; Yashima, 2002, Yashima, Zenuk-Nishide & Shimizu, 2004, see Table 2). Similarly, in the Chinese context, a series of studies were conducted based on MacIntyre et al. 's (1998) model (Peng, 2007; Peng, 2008; Wu, 2008; Peng & Woodrow, 2010; Yu, 2011, see Table 3). Figure 2 in Chapter 2 shows WTC in the micro-and macro-systems of developmental ecological systems (Bronfenbrenner, 1995). For this Chinese L2 WTC study, WTC is placed at the center of the systems. Outside it, there are the learner's self, micro-system of family, classroom, teachers and peers, as well as the macro-system of Chinese culture and globalization.

Meanwhile, L2 WTC theories have been developed along with the emerging studies. To begin with, by reviewing a series of theories and studies in WTC, Matsuoka and Evans (2005) re-conceptualized the L2 WTC model in the East Asian context.

Taking Wen and Clément's (2003) model as an example, Chinese culture plays a huge role in second language learners' WTC. Drawing on Wen and Clément's theoretical model, Wu and Wen's (2009) study researched Chinese students' L2 WTC (see Table 3).

Different from Matsuoka and Evans's (2005) review, Simic and Tanaka's (2008) article categorized the language contexts of current WTC works. WTC theories are first reviewed in their paper and then some re-conceptualizations of L2 WTC are listed. Three types of language texts are later presented. They used two contexts: foreign language contexts in East Asia and the second language contexts in English speaking countries to present studies in L2 WTC. Also, the Japanese language context was discussed as a new perspective. In foreign language contexts, studies of WTC investigated in Korea, China and Japan whereas immersion and study abroad contexts were referred to in the second language contexts. Finally, studies on native English speakers' WTC in using the Japanese language as a second language in Japan were emphasized. In light of the above theories and reviews, the strengths and weaknesses of L2 WTC studies are reviewed (see Tables 2 & 3).

Table 2

Recent L2 WTC Study 1 (outside China): grounded on MacIntyre et al.'s (1998) pyramid model

L2 WTC studies	Strength	Weakness
MacIntyre et al. (2002)	Found positive relation of motivation & attitudes to WTC	Contextual WTC was not studied

Continued

L2 WTC studies	Strength	Weakness
Yashima (2002); Yashima et al. (2004)	Found the relation between motivation and WTC	Contextual WTC was not studied
Kang (2005)	The first one to study contextual WTC	Small sample size
Cao & Philp (2006)	Investigated both trait-like & contextual WTC	Small sample size
Matsubara (2007)	Found the relation of motivation to WTC in Japanese classroom context	Contextual WTC was not studied
de Saint Léger & Storch (2009)	Studied both trait-like & contextual WTC in Australia	Only studied WTC in two classroom contexts: the whole class discussion and small group discussion
MacIntyre & Doucette (2010)	Found an additional predictor of L2 WTC: action control	The predictor may not be applicable to other different cultures, e. g. China
Fushino (2010)	Studied WTC in group work contexts	Covered not all influential factors to WTC
MacIntyre, Burns & Jessome (2011)	Used a new method: a three-step idiodynamic approach (1. an immediate playback of recorded tasks; 2. participants' self-ratings of WTC to form a diagram in a software; 3. discuss for reasons of changes in WTC) to study WTC in tasks	Subjective self-reported ratings

Continued

L2 WTC studies	Strength	Weakness
MacIntyre & Legatto (2011)	Used focused essay to study three different contexts	Contradictory outcomes
Cao (2011)	Found three influential overlapping environmental, individual and linguistic aspects in contextual WTC	Findings cannot be generalized to a specific cultural context since both WTCs were explored among non-native English speakers from different countries

Table 3

Recent L2 WTC Study 2（in China）

Theoretical basis	L2 WTC study	Strength	Weakness
1. MacIntyre et al.'s （1998） pyramid model	Peng (2007)	Found the relation of motivation to WTC in scales among non-BE students	insufficient respondents making it difficult to generalise the outcome to all Chinese L2 students
	Peng (2008)	Studied both trait-like and contextual WTC among non-BE students	Used just two scales of perceived communication competence and WTC
	Wu (2008)	Studied both trait-like and contextual WTC among BE students	Used just two scales of perceived communication competence and WTC

Continued

Theoretical basis	L2 WTC study	Strength	Weakness
2. MacIntyre et al. 's (1998) pyramid model	Peng & Woodrow (2010)	Applied a self-report questionnaire among non-BE students	Contextual WTC was not studied
	Yu (2011)	Studied the effect of teacher support to freshmen and sophomores' contextual WTC	Contextual WTC was not studied
	Peng (2012)	Found WTC factors in micro-, meso-, exo- and macrosystems among 4 non-BE students	Context-specific to non-BE students in China
3. Wen & Clément's (2003) Chinese model	Wu & Wen (2009)	Studied trait-like WTC(DC, motivation, attitudes, societal, risk-taking factors) among BE students	Contextual WTC was not studied and one of WTC factors, tolerance of ambiguity, was omitted in scales

3.3.1　Recent L2 WTC studies outside China

A WTC study was carried out to investigate L1 English speakers in a junior high school in the L2 French-learning immersion education by MacIntyre et al. (2002). The questionnaire used was previously conducted with adults. The influence of language, gender and grade on WTC, anxiety, perceived communication and communication frequency in French and on attitude/motivation variables were measured. The correlation matrix in the study presented that students with positive attitudes and motivation tended to be more willing to communicate, have higher perceived competence, more frequent communication in L2 and lower communication apprehension. It was found that students' L2 WTC, perceived communication competence, and communication frequency increased from Grades 7 to 9. At the same, the anxiety level was steady for the three grades but boys reported more anxiety than girls; however, there was a drop in motivation from Grade 7 to Grade 8. As the programme progresses, the differences between WTC in L1 and L2 narrowed. However, contextual WTC was not investigated in MacIntyre et al. 's (2002) study.

Yashima's (2002) and Yashima et al. 's (2004) studies in both Japan and study-abroad contexts agreed that motivation has an indirect effect on L2 WTC, and thus they emphasized the need of communicating with unfamiliar others while learning English as a second language. Support from host families in the study-abroad programmes turned out to increase students' communicate frequency (Yashima, 2002). The help from host families played a role in guiding and building interpersonal relationships for students; however, in a school context, students had to form interpersonal relationships for themselves. Yashima et al. (2004) pointed out that it should be students' own responsibilities to develop skills and take control of the dynamics of WTC while immersing in a new language environment.

Instead of using questionnaires, Kang (2005) carried out a qualitative study with four Korean male students who studied an English programme in the US, in order to see the dynamic construction of contextual WTC in a L2 during a conversation situation. Data from semi-structured interviews, videotaped conversations and stimulated recalls were analyzed. Categories of emerging themes were formed by identifying first occasions when the participants mentioned their WTC or un-WTC and then the occasion-related affective factors. In order to investigate contextual WTC instead of individual WTC, a cross-case analysis was applied "to build a general explanation that fits each of the individual cases, even though the cases will vary in their details" (Yin, 1994, p. 112). Kang found that three interlinking psychological dimensions, namely, "security, excitement and responsibility" (p. 288) interact with contextual variables such as "topic, interlocutors, and conversational context" (p. 288) to construct contextual WTC in conversations. However, the sampling was very small in Kang's study and only contextual WTC was studied in the research.

With a similarly small number of participants, Cao and Philp (2006) studied eight foreign students' WTC in General English programme in a New Zealand private language school to investigate both trait-like WTC and contextual WTC in L2. Comparing participants' behaviors in whole class, group and dyadic interaction, a self-report survey was implemented to inquire about trait-like WTC while classroom observation and participant interviews were set up to reveal contextual WTC. A series of factors were discovered to impact on WTC in class. That is, "the group size, familiarity with interlocutor (s), interlocutor (s) ' participation, familiarity with topics under discussion, self-discussion, medium of communication and cultural background" (p. 480).

Unlike the former two studies, Matsubara (2007) researched the relationships of L2 motivation, willingness to communicate, and group dynamics in the classroom context in rural Japan with a larger sample size. Similar to MacIntyre et al. (2002), Matsubara (2007) reported the relation of motivation to WTC. Two questionnaires, one for L2 motivation and group dynamics and the other one for L2 WTC, were distributed to 237 university students who were not pursuing BE degree. The findings put forward there is no association between identified group dynamics components of "teaching approach, attitude towards group work, and group cohesion" (p. 216), and WTC; nonetheless, motivational elements in the two types of group dynamics of the student-centered way of instruction and intergroup approach tendency with non-Japanese speakers could significantly benefit students' WTC. However, contextual WTC was not studied in Matsubara's (2007) research.

De Saint Léger and Storch (2009) studied 32 advanced French learners' WTC at an Australian university, with the aim of investigating how learners' perceptions and attitudes towards speaking in whole class and small group discussions influenced WTC in L2 classroom. The study lasted for a semester and data retrieved from week 4 and 12 self-assessment questionnaires as well as focus group interviews showed that learners' perceptions of self affected their WTC.

Classroom observations included two sections. The first section was about students' WTC behavior with the teacher and the section was about students' WTC behavior in pair or group work. Each student was observed by using the classroom observation scheme. Structured interviews involved three parts.

The first part was made of general questions about motivation, anxiety levels and perceived communication competence. The second part was simulated recall questions concerning students' feelings about their own audio-recorded tasks in pair or group works. The last part was individual questions, which asked students to comment on their WTC in pair, group and the whole class situations. Correlation and ANOVA were used to examine the relations between trait-like WTC and the quantified contextual WTC among pair work, group work and the whole class contexts. Qualitative data from the three contexts were then used to supplement the quantitative analysis.

A mismatch was found between trait-like and contextual WTC, suggesting that both trait and contextual WTC influenced a learner's WTC behavior in each of the three contexts. Over time, the more confident the students were in L2 learning, the more willing they were to communicate in L2 in class. However, learners' DC with peers in small groups was varied and motivated by affiliation. However, de Saint Léger and Storch's study only investigated WTC in two classroom contexts: the whole class discussion and small group discussion. Other classroom contexts, such as pair work was not studied.

An additional predictor of WTC was proposed by MacIntyre and Doucette (2010) after studying 238 Canadian high school students. Most of the students were native English speakers and were learning French as a second language. Their model for L2 learners' lack of WTC was grounded in Kuhl's (1994) action control theory which focuses on "preoccupation, hesitation and volatility" (p. 54) as three key components of a person's sense of control. They discovered that not only perceived communication competence and language anxiety were related with WTC, but also the sense of control over action components was involved in the WTC model. The generalizability of this factor to the Chinese context may be questioned because Canadian and Chinese may share different cultural values guiding their actions (Bond & Hwang, 1986). For instance, Chinese people tend to use different types of face-saving behaviors to avoid embarrassment before others.

Solely focusing on WTC in group works, Fushino (2010) investigated the three factors of communication confidence, beliefs about group work as well as willingness to communicate in L2 group works. She used a questionnaire with 729 freshmen in Japan in order to examine the causal relationships of the three factors. The hypothesis was that WTC in L2 group work was affected by beliefs about group work through communication confidence. Beliefs about group work in L2 consisted of three aspects, "beliefs of group work usefulness, negative traditional instruction orientation and positive beliefs about the value of group work" while confidence in L2 group work included "communication apprehension in L2 group work and self-perceived communicative competence" (p. 716). By randomly splitting the collected questionnaires into half, one half of the data were used for model specification of the hypothesis and the other half for confirmation of the model. Structural equation modeling outcomes were consistent with the hypothesis. As the tested model had a relatively simple structure, it could not cover all factors that influence WTC in L2 group work and thus further more detailed and complex constructs were called for to study in this area.

Unlike previous qualitative WTC studies, a new method named an idiodynamic approach was invented by MacIntyre and Legatto (2011) in their WTC study to investigate WTC in tasks. This methodology was built on the basis of stimulated recalls (SR). Eight tasks with both easy and difficult levels were preset for the six participants to conduct. The six female L1 English speakers in Canada were university students aged 19 to 21 who had once been immersed in France and were considered to be fluent in French. The three-step approach in MacIntyre and Legatto's qualitative WTC study of participants' L2 (French) learning involved first an immediate playback of the recorded communication task; then participants self-rated their WTC every second while reviewing their recordings using a developed software and later a diagram was formed; and finally the constructed graph was discussed for reasons of changes in WTC. Applying this methodology, they found that participants' WTC fluctuated with time while different tasks were carried out. Also, linguistic, social, cognitive and affective factors were interconnected to produce WTC. A limitation of the study was that the self-report ratings might turn out to be too subjective.

Another WTC study was also performed in Canada, but with a different qualitative method. Using focused essays, MacIntyre, Burns and Jessome (2011) compared adolescent aged 12—14 French immersion students' descriptions of their willingness and unwillingness to communicate in different contexts. Three types of contexts were being referred to by the participants, involving mostly communications with teachers and friends in school contexts, as well as situations outside the classroom, and the interactions with extended family and what they encountered in media. Seemingly contradictory outcomes emerged as similar willing to communicate and unwilling to communicate situations were generated by participants; however, the authors suggested there were subtle changes to distinguish these situations in a specific context by taking the extents of the authentic nature of communication and students' needs for autonomy, competence and relatedness into account. By recognizing these subtle changes, it was able to improve the ambivalent state of adolescents' WTC and thus moving unwilling to communicate students to WTC.

Considering WTC as a comparatively new individual difference (ID) variable, Cao (2011) regarded the classroom as a micro-system in the macro institutional surrounding from the ecological perspective. For investigating contextual WTC, stimulated recalls, classroom observations and students' reflective journals were used. The participants were from an advanced-level English for academic purposes (EAP) class in New Zealand and most of them were Chinese and Korean.

Data were collected during a three-week pilot study in phase one and a two-week study in phase two. A classroom observation scheme of WTC behaviors mentioned in Cao and Philp's (2006) study above was applied. Student turns in the whole class, group and pair classroom contexts were summed up. Then tokens of WTC behaviors were calculated for each learner. Content analysis was used to analyze data from interviews and journals. Similar to Kang (2005), codes were identified by identifying first occasions when the participants mentioned their WTC or un-WTC (Unwillingness to communicate) and then the occasion-related affective factors.

Findings suggested three influential overlapping environmental, individual and linguistic aspects in dynamic English classrooms. The environmental aspect included topic, task type, interlocutor, teacher and class interactional pattern. The individual part included perceived opportunity to communicate, personality, self-confidence and emotion. The last linguistic filed were composed of language proficiency and reliance on L1. Cao thus called for the English classroom teachers' attention on not only trait WTC, but also the three dimensions influenced contextual WTC. However, the findings cannot be generalized to a specific cultural context since WTC were explored among non-native English speakers from several different countries in Cao's study.

3.3.2 Recent L2 WTC studies in China

3.3.2.1 Studies based on the pyramid WTC model

None of the studies reviewed so far in this chapter has focused on the Chinese context. A range of studies were conducted for researching the extent of WTC and the factors that influence WTC for Chinese college students' English learning based on MacIntyre's (1998) L2 WTC model (Peng, 2007; Peng, 2008; Peng, 2012; Wu, 2008; Peng & Woodrow, 2010; Yu, 2011). In line with the above researchers and with data supporting the idea of a direct association between WTC and motivation, Peng's (2007) study found the relation from motivation to L2 WTC but with a special focus on integrative motivation in the Chinese context. The study site was a college which started to have an intensive English programme to all but medical freshmen in 2004. A questionnaire which involved two measurements, one for L2 WTC inside the classroom and the other one for integrative motivation, were distributed to 174 medical college students. Correlation analysis and multiple regression were used to examine if integrative motivation could predict WTC. The findings turned out that integrative motivation explained a small proportion of variation in WTC. Meanwhile, the motivation factor was the strongest predictor of L2 WTC while attitudes towards different learning contexts could not relate to L2 WTC. A limitation of the study was the insufficient respondents in the programme studied, and thus it is difficult to generalise the outcome to all Chinese L2 students.

Peng (2008) used both qualitative and quantitative methods to see the extent of Chinese college students' willingness to communicate in classrooms in English learning and the factors affecting their willingness to communicate. 118 students from four classes of different grades at a university in Guangzhou Province participated in responding to the questionnaire. The questionnaire consisted of two parts: One part was a five-point Likert scale of MacIntyre's (2001) WTC in L2 inside classroom scale and another part was a six-point scale of self-perceived English proficiency. Then, the researcher invited high and low WTC students from each class to conduct four group semi-structured interviews. In total seventeen students were involved. Finally, one high WTC and one low WTC student were selected from each group to write diaries for two weeks after each English class to reflect what they felt about the classroom interactions with the teacher and peers. The findings suggested that the overall WTC was relatively low but female students' WTC was higher than males'. Positive correlation was found between WTC and self-perceived proficiency but no significant differences of WTC were shown among students in various grades. Content analysis of coded qualitative data listed eight themes that affect WTC in the classroom setting. The eight themes were personal factors of communicative competence, language anxiety, risk-taking, and learner's beliefs as well as social factors of classroom atmosphere, group cohesiveness, teacher support and classroom organisation.

Though similar in using self-perceived communication competence and WTC scales, Wu's (2008) study was different from Peng's (2008) in that Wu investigated BE students rather than non-BE students. 130 BE freshmen were involved in answering the questionnaires. Among them, 39 were male and 91 were female. On average, they had eight years' English learning experience. Firstly, the questionnaire comprised two sections, one of MacIntyre's (1988) self-perceived communication competence scale and the other one of MacIntyre's (1992) and MacIntyre et al. 's (2001) L2 willingness to communicate questionnaire inside and outside classrooms in the four skills of listening, reading, speaking and writing. Secondly, students who obtained the highest and lowest WTC scores in the questionnaire were chosen and their classrooms were observed. The observations lasted for two weeks with eight classes. Field notes included the participants' active involvements in answering the teacher's questions and in group works as well as the length of each active communication time. Thirdly, the four participants in observations were interviewed. It was found that students tended to have relatively low self-perceived communication competence and WTC. Though self-perceived communication competence and WTC was positively correlated, in daily life students' WTC was higher than self-perceived communication competence whereas in classrooms their WTC was lower than self-perceived communication competence. Students' low self-confidence in English learning was affected by their long-term "negative" classroom learning experience and their personalities were also influenced by such classroom learning experience. The main influential factors that affected students' WTC were interlocutor(s), the topic and the context and the feelings of safety and excitement.

Instead of using just two scales of perceived communication competence and WTC, Peng and Woodrow (2010) used a self-report questionnaire to investigate factors that influenced Chinese students' WTC in English learning. Conducting a large scale study of college students' WTC in the English classroom in the Chinese context, Peng and Woodrow constructed a Chinese WTC model with non-Bachelor of English students. The participants in the pilot study were 330 university students from just one of the eight studied universities whereas respondents in the main study were 579 university students from all eight universities. All students were freshmen and sophomores from other disciplines than English, namely, clinical medicine, business administration, engineering communications, and computer science. The model was hypothesized to explore the relationships among WTC in English, communication confidence, motivation, learner beliefs, as well as classroom environment. WTC in English meant two aspects of meaning-and form-focused activities; communication confidence meant communication anxiety and perceived communication competence; motivation meant external regulation, identified regulation and intrinsic motivation; learner beliefs meant perspectives towards English learning and classroom communication; classroom environment meant teacher support, student cohesiveness as well as task orientation. A two-phase procedure was carried out to first pilot the questionnaire items through exploratory factor analysis for reducing items as well as to identify the factor structure, and then the main study validated the instrument through confirmatory factor analysis and the hypothesized structural model was tested using SEM.

The outcome can be seen in Figure 7 below. Dotted lines were data-driven paths added after modifying the hypothesized model. Undotted lines were those in the hypothesized model. The results showed that classroom environment was the predictor of WTC, communication confidence, learner beliefs, and motivation. Motivation was indirectly related with WTC through confidence while the learner beliefs factor had direct relations with motivation and communication confidence respectively.

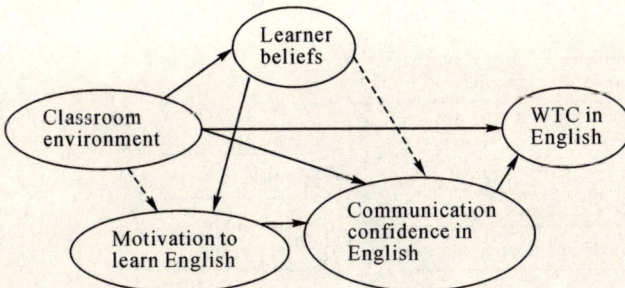

Figure 7. Structural model of WTC in English in Chinese EFL classroom (Peng & Woodrow, 2010).

A recent study result, Yu (2011) supported MacIntyre et al.'s (1998) WTC model with a special emphasis on teacher immediacy on Chinese students' WTC in spoken English learning. Teacher immediacy, which refers to the teacher's verbal or nonverbal communication behaviors for creating physical and psychological closeness with students, is actually teacher support in Wen and Clément's (2003) model (Yu, 2011). In order to probe into the relationships among communication comprehension (CA), self-perceived communication competence (SPCC), teacher immediacy and L2 WTC in spoken English (WTC_E), as well as affective variables of integrativeness, attitudes toward the learning situation (ATLS), motivation and instrumental orientation, questionnaires were distributed to 234 sophomores and juniors at a university in China. The final modified path model is presented in the following Figure 8. The figure shows that teacher immediacy and the other three affective variables all directly related with motivation; CA, ATLS and motivation indirectly influenced WTC through SPCC; and also motivation indirectly affected WTC through CA. However, contextual WTC was not studied in both Yu's (2011) and Peng and Woodrow's (2010) research.

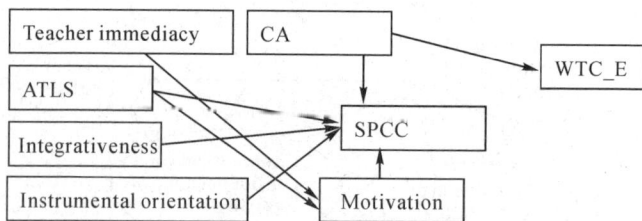

Figure 8. A Chinese WTC model founded by Yu (2011).

Peng (2012) used qualitative instead of quantitative instruments to study four non-BE students' WTC in English language classrooms at a comprehensive university in southern China. High and low WTC students in a previously conducted WTC scale in first- and second-year classes were selected by using the extreme or deviant case sampling strategy (Dörnyei, 2007). During seven months, semi-structured interviews, non-participant classroom observations and learning journals were conducted to explore students' individual and contextual WTC. Using Bronfenbrenner's (1995) eco-systems model, Peng found six WTC factors of learner beliefs, motivation, cognitive, linguistic, affective factors and classroom environment in the micro-system. Also, the effects of other eco-systems: meso-system (past learning experience &. participation in extracurricular activities), exo-system (the relationship between classroom setting and curriculum design and evaluation criteria), and macro-system (social, educational and cultural factors) on WTC in classrooms were suggested. She concluded that the ecological findings of Chinese EFL students' WTC were consistent with Cao's (2011) findings in Section 3.3.1. However, Peng's study was context-specific to non-BE students in China. Other factors in the eco-systems, such as family can also influence learners' WTC.

3.3.2.2 *Studies based on the Chinese WTC model*

Modifying MacIntyre et al.'s (1998) model of WTC in terms of Chinese culture and philosophy, Wen and Clément (2003) presented a Chinese conceptualization of WTC (see Figure 3 in Chapter 2). In order to move from DC to WTC (from the second to the third layer in MacIntyre et al.'s model), a

Chinese learner of English has to overcome four categories of factors in three layers Ⅳ, Ⅴ and Ⅵ of MacIntyre et al. 's model. The first category includes "teacher support" and "group cohesiveness", the state of remaining in a group; the second one comprises "risk-taking" and "tolerance of ambiguity"; the third one consists of "affiliation", the sense of togetherness within a group as well as "task-orientation", focus on one's ability and sense of self-worth, and also on public recognition; and the last one is made up of "inhibited monitor" and "positive expectation of evaluation". Considering task-orientation, Matsuoka and Evans (2005) noted that it is actually controlled in the classroom settings. Then, an inhibited monitor is expressed in that the more competent the students feel about their English learning, the less correction they will utilize. In addition, Wen and Clément (2003) mentioned that Chinese students tend to be monitor over-users, where the monitor is learners' observed tendency to "self-correct their production based on their conscious application of rules they have learned" (p. 32). Nonetheless, what Wen and Clément displayed is a theoretical framework rather than study findings of WTC in the Chinese context and the interrelationships between variables and WTC are not all noted. At the end of the article, Wen and Clément call for studies using both quantitative and qualitative methods.

Based on Wen and Clément's WTC model, Wu and Wen (2009) conducted a quantitative study of 242 BE students in three Chinese universities. The results first showed that participants' DC was higher than WTC. Using a six-point Likert scale questionnaire and computing bivariate correlation and multivariate regression in SPSS 13. 0, direct and indirect causal relations to WTC were pinned down (see Figure 9). They found that DC, motivational orientation, and risk-taking in personality factors directly affected WTC. Indirectly, DC related to WTC through risk-taking and motivational orientation; societal context connected with WTC through risk-taking; affective perceptions linked with WTC through risk-taking and motivational orientation. However, the tolerance of ambiguity variable was excluded from their questionnaire because of its low reliability coefficient (Cronbach $\alpha = 0.422$). Also, contextual WTC was not studied.

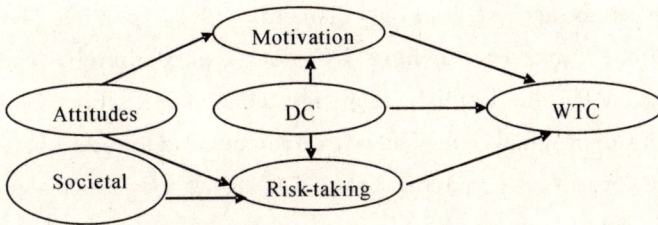

Figure 9. Path diagram on relations of variables influencing WTC (Wu & Wen, 2009).

This project proposes to use qualitative studies in conjunction with a replication of the survey study to examine the interaction of personal and contextual factors on student WTC in Chinese higher education. The Chinese L2 WTC model is suitable to be used in this study to investigate both trait-like and contextual L2 WTC since it is an extension of MacIntyre et al.'s (1998) WTC theories in the Chinese classroom context. The next section will take a closer look at factors in Wen and Clément's conceptual framework as well as challenge the model regarding the claimed collectivistic outlook of the Chinese.

3.4 The Chinese WTC model

3.4.1 Factors in the Chinese WTC model

3.4.1.1 DC and WTC

In Wen and Clément's (2003) WTC model, desire to communicate with a specific person (DC) is the starting point for WTC. DC and WTC are distinct in that the former is "a deliberate choice or preference" while the latter "emphasizes the readiness to act" (Wen & Clément, 2003, p. 25). DC is universal; however, owning DC does not definitely lead to having WTC in English language classrooms. For Chinese learners of English, they have to overcome additional obstacles in the process of moving from DC to WTC, such as the possibility of losing face in front of others. As mentioned above, the Chinese self is related with others. Thus, Chinese tend to be sensitive to evaluations from significant others for the purpose of saving face and being comfortable within their own group culture; they are also very cautious while interacting with outgroup cultures (Wen & Clément, 2003). Though students can have high DC in English learning, they may be unwilling to communicate in classrooms due to these other-directed factors.

3.4.1.2 Personality

Research into WTC in language learning has found that personal characteristics such as "risk-taking" and "tolerance of ambiguity" are important contributors to WTC (Wen & Clément, 2003, p. 25). Risk-taking and tolerance of ambiguity are the two personality factors which seem to be affectively related while considering the collectivistic cultural influences on the Chinese. Risk-taking is "any consciously, or unconsciously controlled behavior with a perceived uncertainty about its outcome" (Trimpop, 1994, p. 9). The features of tolerance of ambiguity are "novelty, complexity, insolubility and unstructuredness" (Wen &. Clément, 2003, p. 30) and in the presence of ambiguous learning situations, learners' attitudes differ and their behaviors vary. Personality is an enduring factor in MacIntyre et al.'s (1998) WTC model. The introversion/extraversion personality trait in "the Big Five"—"neuroticism, extraversion, openness, agreeableness and conscientiousness" (Matthews &. Deary, 1998, p. 27), was drawn by McCrosky and Richmond (1990) to build WTC theory in L1. They claimed that extraverts are more willing to communicate than introverts. Kaya (1995) found that students' personality in the introversion/extraversion dimension was connected with their active class participation. Studies on WTC concerning the introversion or extraversion personality trait were conducted by MacIntyre et al. (1999) and MacIntyre (1994). Results show that introversion influences WTC through communication apprehension and perceived competence (MacIntyre et al., 1999), while extraversion influences WTC through self-esteem, communication apprehension and perceived competence (MacIntyre, 1994). Moreover, extroverted students tend to be more risk-taking and more tolerant of ambiguities (Wen &. Clément, 2003).

Wen and Clément noted that Chinese learners are less likely to take risks and less tolerant of ambiguities in language learning classes. Chinese learners of English will act submissively (i. e., not

actively speak out) to minimize the risk of losing face (Wen &
Clément, 2003). There is a well-known Confucius saying, "Don't
pretend to know what you don't know; know what one really
understands." That means guessing is also not valued in Chinese
culture, as tolerance of ambiguities implies the knowledge is not fully
mastered by the learner.

3.4.1.3   Societal context

A second language learner's WTC interacts with the societal
context (McGroarty, 1998; Dörnyei, 2001). First, to
successfully acquire a second language, a learner must master
language skills and rules and the behavioral and cognitive
features of the target sociocultural community. In this case, it is
essential to understand the importance of the social dimension of
L2 motivation (Dörnyei, 2001). However, a second language
may be learned in diverse contexts. According to McGroarty
(1998), different social environments can influence L2
competence differently and can also result in various degrees of
motivational intensity. Thus, it is vital to take contextual
differences into account when considering L2 motivation. The
social influence on attitudes has often been neglected in previous
studies in language learning (Terry et al., 1999). Nevertheless,
studies of attitudes should focus on both individual and societal
levels (Dörnyei, 2001). Therefore, L2 attitudes should be
considered in the societal context.

Societal context includes "teacher support" and "group
cohesiveness" (Wen & Clément, 2003, p. 25) as well as
students' interactions with teachers and peers inside the class.
Group cohesiveness in Chinese contexts implies a strong
conformity to the group and reduces student WTC for fear of

disrupting the harmony of the collective (Wen & Clément, 2003). Furthermore, in China, a great many teachers are strongly in charge of activities and expect a submissive or passive way of learning from their students (Geng, 2007). However, Geng's view is based on the speculation of the traditional Chinese culture.

Teacher support can influence group cohesiveness while constructing the societal context. Hamm et al. (2011) found that the students in classes where teachers were more attuned to group work reported improved views of the school social learning environment. They studied the effect of a teacher training programme on rural teachers' attunement to student social dynamics and school experiences. Teacher attunement is an aspect of teacher involvement and teacher involvement is the extent to which teachers "take time for, express affection toward, enjoy interaction with, are attuned to, and dedicate resources to their students" (Skinner & Belmont, 1993, p. 573). Teacher attunement refers to teacher support in students' social-affective domains and it can lead to better student engagement (Hamm et al. , 2011). In intervention schools, there were fourteen teachers with training on social dynamics and early adolescent adjustment. In the control group, twelve untrained teachers were chosen. 225 students and the 26 teachers' views towards peer groups were compared through structured observations of teachers as well as questionnaires with students. However, Hamm et al. 's study of the influence of teacher attunement to students' peer group affiliation is limited to a middle school transition context.

3.4.1.4 Motivation

Motivation consists of "affiliation" as well as "task-orientation" (Wen & Clément, 2003, p. 25). Affiliation is the sense of togetherness within a group. Task-orientation focuses on one's ability and sense of self-worth, and also on public recognition (Wen & Clément, 2003). In this sense, perceived communication competence and anxiety are two areas of task-orientation. Matsuoka and Evans (2005) noted that task-orientation is actually a type of personal control in the classroom setting. It is widely believed that confidence in one's abilities can enhance motivation (Dörnyei, 2001). Centinkaya (2005) noted that communicative self-confidence in learning a L2 can be examined through perceived communication competence and anxiety.

Relating the two aspects of societal context with motivation in the Chinese context, group cohesiveness seems to be linked with affiliation whereas teacher support is in line with task-orientation. Chinese learners of English tend not to have a warm feeling and sense of togetherness while affiliated to an unfamiliar group in classroom interactions (Wen & Clément, 2003). Students may be afraid of losing face and getting disapproval from the teacher if they fail to finish their tasks (Yu & Gu, 1990). Substantial WTC studies on motivation have witnessed the indirect influence of motivation on WTC (e.g. Yashima, 2002; Yashima, Zenuk-Nishide & Shimizu, 2004) as well as a direct relation between motivation and L2 WTC (MacIntyre et al., 2002; Matsubara, 2007; Peng, 2007).

3.4.1.4.1 Instrumental motivation in China

A number of researchers have shown that motivation influences students' use of second language strategies, the amount of input they received in the second language learning process, performances in course-related examinations, general second language proficiency levels, and how long the second language skills can be maintained once the language study is over (Ely, 1986; Gardner, 2000; Scarcella & Oxford, 1992).

Schmidt & Watanabe (2001) found that motivation influences strategy use and preferences towards different kinds of classroom activities. 2,089 learners of five foreign languages of Mandarin Chinese, Filipino, French, Japanese and Spanish were surveyed at the University of Hawaii. The factor analyzed questionnaire consisted of motivational factors of value, expectancy, motivational strength, competitiveness and cooperativeness. It turned out that value, motivational strength and cooperation had impacts on learners' strategy use and pedagogical preferences. Moreover, motivation influenced the application of cognitive and metacognitive strategies, as well as pedagogical preferences of challenging activities.

The existence of integrative motivation in Asian learners of English was rejected and strong instrumental motivation was witnessed in Warden and Lin's (2000) study. The study investigated different motivational groups, of integrative, instrumental and a required motivation. A required motivation was added in the study as English language learning is mandatory in Taiwan. Questionnaires were distributed to over 2,000 non-BA students in two institutions in Taiwan. The preliminary findings with 500 participants in one Taiwan institution were reported. Exploratory factor analysis revealed the existence of distinct motivational groups. Strong required motivation and instrumental motivation were found. The authors suggested that the disappearance of integrative motivational groups was due to the direct borrowing of the western ESL classroom techniques.

The existence of Chinese students' integrative motivation was evidenced by Liu (2007) with the use of the modified Gardner (1985) and Clément et al. (1994) scales, though more instrumental motivation was presented than integrative motivation.

3.4.1.4.2 *Language anxiety*

Sparks et al. (2000) suggested that foreign language anxiety is a result rather than a cause of poor achievement in foreign language learning. A third variable of cognitive-linguistic disability causes poor achievement and then leads to foreign language anxiety. Horwitz (2000) argued that for some language learners the third variable is not evident, implying that foreign language anxiety can directly interfere with language learning. Horwitz's perspective is widely believed by language learners and teachers (MacIntyre, 1995a, 1995b; Spielberger, 1966).

Anxiety reduces once learners become more competent and obtain more positive English learning experience (MacIntyre & Gardner, 1989). Nevertheless, Zhang (2011) put forward the view that both language proficiency and cognitive factors can affect anxiety. Zheng (2008) also suggested the studies on language anxiety shifted from behavioral to psychodynamics, regarding anxiety as an inhibiting factor for L2 learners. A relationship between anxiety and perceived communication competence was found (Liu & Jackson, 2008; Pichette, 2009).

Liu (2006) took a close look at Chinese learners' anxiety in English language learning. The purpose of the study was to find out non-BE students' anxiety and these students have English proficiency at three different levels. Instruments of survey, observations, reflective journals and interviews were used. Four research outcomes were uncovered. Firstly, as a whole, more than one third of students at each of the three proficiency levels reported a feeling of anxiety while speaking English in the classroom. Secondly, students with higher proficiency tended to feel less anxious. Thirdly, the most anxious context was to speak English alone or do presentations unprepared when facing the whole class or to a teacher, especially for less competent learners of English, whereas the least anxious circumstance was to conduct pair work and group discussions. Lastly, students tended to feel less anxious using English in speech communication with more exposure to spoken English.

However, students with higher proficiency in English may not necessarily tend to be less anxious in English classrooms. Brown (2008) discovered the reason can be ascribed to students' low self-confidence, feeling of shame and inferiority. An additional reason might lay in a perfectionist tendency. It was found that anxious language learners cannot be easily happy about their currently held academic achievements (Gregersen & Horwitz, 2002).

3.4.1.4.3 Anxiety reduction

How to make task topics in BE students' English classes reduce their uneasiness in speaking English is an issue that needs attention (Liu & Jackson, 2008; Timina & Butler, 2011). Seventy BE juniors at a university in Taiwan participated in

Timina and Butler's (2011) study. Speaking anxiety and unwillingness to communicate were two prominent signs of these students while speaking English in their English classes. It was found that the some topics, such as private life, indeed embarrassed BE students in English classes. False impression of assuming these students lack motivation in learning English can be imprinted on their instructors; nonetheless, this issue appears to be rooted in the Chinese culture. In order to construct supportive classroom contexts to enhance BE students' WTC, it seems essential for English teachers to bring forth culturally-appropriate task topics to back up their students' spoken English learning.

In a similar vein, Liu and Jackson (2008) found that many items in the interest variable can predict Chinese undergraduates' unwillingness to communicate and their English learning anxiety. A survey was carried out with 547 non-BE freshmen by Liu and Jackson (2008). They researched not only the unwillingness to communicate, but also anxiety of Chinese learners of English in English language classrooms. An outcome collected by using a scale with seventy items showed that though a large number of students were willing to become involved in interpersonal conversations, many of them were afraid of taking risk in speaking English in class.

3.4.1.5 Attitudes

Attitude perspectives are made up of an "inhibited monitor" and "positive expectation of evaluation" (Wen & Clément, 2003, p. 25). An inhibited monitor is reflected in the fact that the more competent the students feel about their English learning, the less correction they will utilize. In this sense, a student's high perceived communication competence can express the low extent of inhibited monitor. Positive expectation of evaluation is derived from the face-protection orientation and a student's self-esteem increases when he or she gets positive remarks from others.

Attitudes have been long regarded as an important component in foreign and second language learning (Smith, 1971; Dörney, 2003). The construction of attitudes, either for a teacher or for a learner of a foreign language, has been conceptualized as involving several steps from cognitive component (the perception about a situation) to the affective component (the good or bad feeling towards the cognitive component) to the evaluative component (evaluate the situation) and finally translated into the behavioral component (the action showing one's attitude) (Smith, 1971).

Dörnyei (2001) suggested the necessities of integrating individualistic and societal perspectives to research L2 attitudes. Individual Chinese students tend to "self-correct their production based on their conscious application of rules they have learned" (Dörnyei, 2001, p. 32). The concern for judgments from significant others puts pressures on Chinese L2 learners (Yu, 1990). Also, many pay attention to the correct forms in language learning so as to avoid social embarrassment (Wen & Clément, 2003). Hence, Chinese cultural priorities are likely to reduce WTC, a significant potential explanation for the "silent" speaker.

Positive correlation was found between academic performance and learning attitudes in China for students who were learning English as a second language at the tertiary level

(Liu，Chang & Gan，2010). Liu，Chang and Gan's (2010) study examined the current so-called 1990s-generation non-Bachelor of English students' attitudes and their academic performance in college English in China. A report stated that since 2008，those students who were born in the 1990s had become the main component of the college students (Wuhan University，2008). The report also noted that 1990s-generation students have different personalities when compared with 1970s-and 1980s-generation students. That is，1990s-generation students' tended to be more independent，mature，confident，enthusiastic，and planned than 1970s-and 1980s-generation students. Using a self-report five point Likert questionnaire，81 valid questionnaires were obtained. Meanwhile，students' English scores at the end of the previous semester were collected. It was found that academic scores in English and learning attitudes were positively correlated. Also，no differences between male and female students regarding learning attitudes and English sores were found. Since the sample size was quite small，generalisation of the outcome to other contexts may be improper.

A much larger scale of study on students' attitudes was conducted by Ma，Zhang and Hu (2004). They tried to find out what reasons can be attributed to some college students' "unwillingness to learn" attitude. With regard to working hard，the questionnaire study of 1,000 students at 12 universities and colleges in Hangzhou，Zhejiang Province in 2003 showed that 64.2% students mentioned it was mainly lack of learning aims and motivations that resulted in their reluctance to be hard working. The authors concluded that college students' unwillingness to learn attitudes resulted from this lack of learning aims and motivation. The state-regulated top-down curriculum organization, old fashioned teaching content, stiff classroom instruction without communication and no strict requirements from universities and teachers for students were reasons behind this attitudes. However, the study outcome covered the overall picture of all courses in college rather than just English courses. It may be improper to generalize the results to English courses.

3.4.2 Challenged collectivistic outlook of the Chinese

However, Wen and Clément's (2003) Chinese conceptualization of L2 WTC faced a challenge since all the guess work in the model was based on so-called traditional collectivistic outlook of the Chinese and need to be tested. Some researchers challenged the traditional view regarding Chinese learners of English in classroom contexts and the so-called collective Chinese culture (Garrott, 1995; Shi, 2006). In Garrott's (1995) semi-structured and open-ended questionnaire study of 512 undergraduate students at 15 Chinese colleges or universities, the findings indicated that BE and non-BE students differed in their conceptions toward English language learning, such as manifesting in the level of anxiety. Meanwhile, she found that the students tended to be individualistic from verbatim student comments. A presumption of the reason resulting in students' move towards individualism is the impact of globalization after the reform and opening-up policy in China, which largely influences students' perspectives on English language learning and gradually to some extent eases their nervousness in classroom learning with the introduction and development of communicative language learning imported from western countries.

Consistent with Garrott, Shi (2006) later posed a question regarding the current cultural influence on Chinese students' English language learning asking whether the learners of English were merely successors to Confucianism or a new generation. Through investigation of 400 Chinese middle-school students in 2003, the questionnaire data revealed that the students showed different features in English learning when compared with the stereotyped Chinese cultural image of being completely passive, quiet, submissive and disciplined. The findings suggested these students were active and preferring to be more interactive with their teachers in classrooms. Shi concluded that the emergence of the new generation was attributable to rapid social changes in China. Nevertheless, some issues remain to affect Chinese learners of English; for instance, the influence of examinations to students' view of English learning. Cheng (2008) reviewed the English language testing in China and named it the key to success. Over the past decades, English language tests, which are vital to show academic success and success in life for many English learners in China, have been administered and developed for billions of English learners across the nation.

3.5 *Conclusion*

In this chapter, a historical review of the literature and studies on willingness to communicate (WTC) in the first language as well as the second language are first presented.

Then, the Chinese WTC model is emphasized and the WTC factors of DC, WTC, personality, societal context, motivation and attitudes in the Chinese culture are probed into and a challenge of the model is mentioned concerning the changed collectivism in China. The study in this book would fill the gap of reviewed literatures in using all variables in the Chinese L2 WTC model to investigate BE students' WTC and suggesting pedagogical changes to enhance students' WTC in speaking in English language lessons in China. The next chapter will turn to the methodology part of the book regarding WTC in the Chinese culture.

Chapter 4
Methodology

4.1 Research design

This project mixed quantitative and qualitative research methods. Mixing methods presumes that the philosophic dichotomy of quantitative (e. g. , positivistic, theory-driven, statistical analysis) and qualitative (e. g. , interpretive, data-driven, researcher analyzed) methods can be overcome by judiciously mixing different methods to explore complementary aspects of a research problem (Hammersley, 1992; Johnson & Onwuegbuzie, 2004). This approach requires successfully sequencing different studies in order to build an integrated understanding in which the strengths of each method are used partially to compensate for weaknesses in other methods and more importantly to answer distinctive but related research questions.

While there are multiple options as to how to coordinate quantitative and qualitative methods, Creswell (2008) viewed an explanatory mixed methods design as the most popular pattern. In an explanatory design, the general picture of the research problem is obtained from a quantitative technique (e. g. , a factor analyzed survey), then, qualitative studies (e. g. , interviews, observations, or document interpretation) provide detailed insights that seek to "refine, extend, or explain the general picture" (p. 560). Figure 10 shows the mixed research design in the case study.

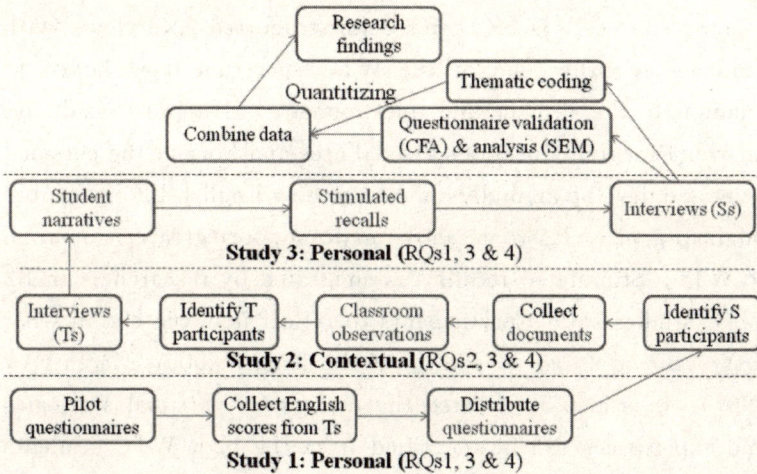

Figure 10. Mixed methods research design in the Chinese WTC case study.

Three sequential studies were planned for this project during academic years 2010—2011 to address the research questions. Study One used a student self-report, factor analyzed survey questionnaire to establish baseline values for the WTC model variables in a single site (i. e. , a Chinese university) to answer Research Questions One, Three and Four at the personal level. Studies Two and Three were designed after the completion of Study One. Study Two analyzed documents, classroom observations, and semi-structured interviews with teachers to examine in more detailed questions related to the pedagogical contextual factors implemented in English teaching classrooms in the same site to answer Research Questions Two to Four at the contextual level. Study Three examined in detail the personal life experiences of students who were identified by their instructors as being high or low in WTC. By examining student narratives, stimulated recalls (SR) and semi-structured interviews with students at either end of the WTC spectrum it is hoped to triangulate the teacher and questionnaire self-report results to answer Research Questions One, Three and Four at the personal level and develop an understanding of how English L2 instructors might organize classroom activities to support greater transition to WTC. Stimulated recalls, as suggested by researchers in L2 WTC studies, allow participants to reflect immediately on what just occurred (Cao & Philp, 2006; Kang, 2005; MacIntyre, 2007). It is also anticipated that successful personal strategies and experiences can be identified from the high WTC students that could be used to guide low WTC students into developing greater WTC.

Research methods interacted with each other in the three studies. In Study Two, the analysis of documents served to form the criteria for coding classroom observations. Teachers' semi-structured interviews sought to identify reasons behind what had been observed in English lessons. In Study Three, student narratives of past and present learning experiences partially explained their WTC in classroom observations. Stimulated recalls ask students to reflect on their feelings about what has happened in classroom observations. Student interviews investigated individual responses of WTC model variables in questionnaires in Study One in more depth. The personal factors found in Study One and Study Three were combined with the investigated contextual factors in Study Two to form a synthesized L2 WTC pyramid model.

A challenge of integrating quantitative and qualitative studies is that incompatible outcomes may arise from the two types of data (Harris & Brown, 2010; Yardley & Bishop, 2008). Harris and Brown (2010) noted that quantitative and qualitative data are at best complementary to each other and incompatible outcomes can still arise. Using both structured questionnaires and semi-structured interviews to the same participants, they suggested there will be a discrepancy between quantitative and qualitative data. One proper way to minimize this discrepancy at the data analysis stage can be to first analyze the two data sets separately and then compare the results to see if similar findings emerge. Taking a sample selection in qualitative studies as an example, those students reported to be high or low WTC students by teachers may not respond in the same way as they did in a questionnaire. Yin (2006) pointed out a way to resolve this kind of conflict in a case study is either to revisit the former resource or to bring in a third resource.

Since there are only 400 candidates in the case study site enrolled in Bachelor of English programmes, the questionnaires were distributed to all of the BE students at the university. The high likelihood of responses was controlled to keep an individual student's answers private. Students were not allowed to talk in class while answering the questionnaire. The environment did not allow or create much interaction between BEE and BBE students then there was a low likelihood of influence. Also, there was no showing of responses to the teacher or other people. The probability of influence was actually low.

For obtaining qualitative data, teachers were asked to identify 3 students with high WTC and 3 students with low WTC from each type of BE students. Teachers selected high and low WTC students based on the students' inclination to speak in English lessons. Maximal variation sampling (Creswell, 2008; Patton, 2002) was applied and participants were selected according to their differences in grades, genders, extent of WTC and specified majors. These 12 students were asked to identify and describe the teaching practices of two teachers who helped them to have high WTC and/or who discouraged their WTC.

4.2 The case study approach

This project adopts a case study strategy approach because it allows the collection of both quantitative and qualitative data and is an important means of probing into differences within a common setting (Mills, Wiebe & Durepos, 2010). Moreover, case studies can move research from artificial or abstract contexts to an understanding of social phenomena in real-life situations (Yin, 2009). A further advantage of the case study is its increased manageability; the scope of the study is defined by the limits of the case parameters.

The nature of case study is "idiographic" (p. 69), that is, dealing with individual cases in their own unique contexts, and while this reduces overall generalizability to all situations from which the case is drawn (Yin, 2009), the potential remains for developing new hypotheses and insights that can be tested in subsequent large-scale studies. Thus, a case study can help form new theories in a knowledge domain. Investigating Chinese BE students' WTC in a single case study site, it is possible to find out what personal and contextual factors hinder and enable their L2 WTC in spoken English inside classrooms. Though the outcome may not be able to be applied in all Chinese contexts, the factors found can draw pedagogical implications and these factors and implications can be tested in other contexts for researching L2 WTC.

Selection of a case is an important factor. The selected case must reasonably reflect characteristics of the population of similar cases; otherwise it will be so idiographic that it will have little potential applicability beyond the borders of its own parameters. A good case then is one which shares many important attributes with similar organizations or settings. In this study, the university site selected (30, 266 full-time students) (Liu, 2012) is one of a large population of provincial Chinese universities offering English language instruction for both teaching and commerce applications. Though no detailed statistics can be found as to how many Chinese universities provide both BEE and BBE programmes, approximately 500 universities established BE programme according to the business direction (*Twenty-first Century*, 2007) and at least the 98 normal universities have BEE programmes (Apollo, 2009). A final reason for using the case study method is that the researcher is an insider of a Chinese university and so access and permission to carry out the study was relatively easy to obtain. Though it is hard to maintain objectivity in insider research and the validity can be threatened by a researcher's biases, researching as an insider is better than an outsider since it can add richness, honesty, fidelity and authenticity to the obtained information (Rooney, 2005). According to Rooney, for instance, an insider owns a wealth of privy knowledge that an outsider is not able to have. Furthermore, the direct study of the university's own students and teaching will have strong practical application benefit for the site itself. Access approval to the case site university was obtained from its Teaching Affairs Office.

4.3   Research setting and participants

China's normal universities usually have two types of English language majors; that is, learning to become a teacher of English (e. g. , Bachelor of English Education or Bachelor of Education (Normal)) and learning to use English in commercial contexts (e. g. , Bachelor of English or Bachelor of Business English). A major role of a normal university in China's higher education system is to produce teachers; thus, normal universities assume the primary responsibility of educating in-service teachers and preparing pre-service teachers of English, among all other school subjects. However, consistent with recent globalization processes, the current education market in China needs diverse graduates who are competent in English language in order to meet the country's socio-economic development. Additionally, Chinese universities offer degrees in English in commerce-related areas in order to enhance their own competitiveness and comprehensive stature.

It should be noted that candidates for the teaching and commerce-related English degrees generally have different levels of academic performance on the Chinese National Entrance Examinations. Students entering teaching programmes tend to have higher entrance examination scores and this may be a factor in not only the English teaching contexts but also student WTC. Another distinction lies in the relative requirement that the chosen career requires the use of English. It is clear that teachers of English plan to use English once they enter their careers; however, the probability that business graduates will actually need to use English is not so clearly established. Some business graduates may need spoken English, for instance, working as translators in business sectors; however, others may work in business sectors where English is only needed in the written form.

This case study investigated BE students' WTC in spoken English in English language classrooms in Wenzhou University, Zhejiang Province, China. According to the 2010 ranking list of the top 600 universities in China, Wenzhou University ranks number 285 (China University Alumni Association, 2010). As a comprehensive city-level university, it is in the south of Zhejiang Province. The university is not a normal university but did absorb a local normal college (i. e. , teacher education institute) in 2006. Currently, the university has approximately 400 BE students with almost an even split between BEE (Bachelor of Educational English) and BBE (Bachelor of Business English) students. All BE students started learning English at least from middle schools, which means six years before entering the university. Both BEE and BBE students are required to study general English courses, such as integrated English courses. The differences are that BEE students also have to study specialized

73

courses in not only English linguistics, literature and culture, but also in other teaching related modules, such as education, psychology and technologies; whereas, BBE students take business English classes. Additionally, BEE and BBE students can choose selective courses from each other's compulsory English courses to study.

4.4 *Instruments*

Instruments used in this research are questionnaires, curriculum related documents (see Section 4.4.2), student narratives, classroom observations, stimulated recalls (SR), and semi-structured interviews with teachers and students. Questionnaires were used to survey student personal factors, then inspection of teaching documents, followed by classroom observations and semi-structured teacher interviews, were used to study the contextual factors of learning. Student narratives, stimulated recalls and semi-structured interviews with students were used to further elucidate student responses to contextual factors. The goal was to suggest pedagogical strategies that would maximize WTC in English language classrooms for all BE students in the case study site. The following sections will explain the application of each instrument in this research in detail.

4.4.1 *Questionnaires*

Items for the questionnaire were selected to explore the various important facets of research into WTC. Eight factors had been selected; namely, academic performance, WTC, DC, personality, affiliation, anxiety, perceived communication competence, and positive expectation of evaluation. Except for the self-report WTC factor and academic scores, all the other variables had been adapted from previously published scales and will be depicted in the following sections. Modifications were made by either transforming five-point rating scales into six-point positively-packed agreement scales (Brown, 2004) or by reducing items in later pilot studies. The WTC questionnaire (see Appendix A) was piloted through EFA (exploratory factor analysis) to ascertain the validity of the translated scales. In addition, personal information was obtained in the questionnaires. Because it was possible to obtain students' actual academic English scores directly from university records, only the other seven factors were described:

(1) WTC. To explore WTC, students were asked to rate their willingness to communicate in a range of plausible contexts according to the anticipated requirements implied by the teaching syllabi of each degree type. Questions for English Education majors were designed according to the requirements for being a teacher of English, with special attention paid to accurate pronunciation and conversation skills, as BEE students were expected to have solid English competences and communicate with students skillfully in English language classrooms. In contrast, BBE students were presented contexts in which they might have to practically apply spoken English in business contexts. For example, students were asked to indicate their willingness to communicate as to "make a speech on a familiar topic in English" (for BEE students) and "have a job interview in English" (for BBE students).

Students were given a positively-packed agreement rating scale with two negative and four positive choices (i. e. , 1＝strongly unwilling; 2＝mostly unwilling; 3＝slightly willing; 4＝moderately willing; 5＝mostly willing; and 6＝strongly willing). A positively-packed rating scale is recommended when respondents can plausibly be expected to be positive towards constructs (Brown, 2004), which is the case here as students were expected to be positive about their ability to apply English in their future careers. Meanwhile, Chinese students expect positive evaluations from others (Wen & Clément, 2003) and thus it may be possible that students in the study tend to agree with the statements while responding questionnaires. In this case, the four positive choices may provide more distinctions concerning students' responses to a statement.

(2) DC. Four items were adapted from the 'desire to learn English scale (Matsubara, 2007) and a six-point Likert scale was employed ranging from 6＝very strongly agree to 1＝very strongly disagree. The scale is then positively packed with: 1＝very strongly disagree; 2＝mostly disagree; 3＝slightly agree; 4＝moderately agree; 5＝mostly agree; 6＝strongly agree. Using an existing reliable scale is easier and more appropriate than developing one (Creswell, 2008). Also, the more the existing scale is used, the better statistics and interpretation the questionnaire will obtain.

(3) Personality. Six items were adapted from Centinkaya (2005) to examine extrovert-introvert dimensions of personality. A nine-point semantic differential or bipolar scale is used. If a question is worded with many response categories ordered on a continuum, a student may arbitrarily choose one; but if the number of response categories is reduced, there is a danger of

losing details (De Vaus, 2000). de Vaus suggested an approach to deal with a question with many response categories is to simplify the number of response categories by converting them to a numerical scale. Respondents select a number from one to nine to state the degree to which they endorse the term at either end of the continuum.

(4) Affiliation. Five items of "group cohesion" were also adapted from Matsubara (2007). A six-point scale is employed ranging from 6＝ very strongly agree to 1＝very strongly disagree. The scale is then positively packed with: 1＝very strongly disagree; 2＝mostly disagree; 3＝slightly agree; 4＝moderately agree; 5＝mostly agree; 6＝strongly agree.

(5) Anxiety. Six items of "anxiety" in terms of communication apprehension were adapted from MacIntyre and Doucette (2010). A hundred percent scale will be utilized ranging from 0＝completely relaxed to 100＝extremely nervous. Equal distances between stopping points were ten. According to de Vaus (2002), the longer scale allows for finer differences. For instance, using a ten-point scale can detect greater real discriminations between people than distributing on a five-point scale (Alwin, 1997). Also, the number of response categories can be simplified in a hundred percent scale with stopping points (de Vaus, 2002).

(6) Perceived communication competence. Six items of "perceived communication competence" were adapted from Cetinkaya (2005). A hundred percent scale were utilized ranging from 0＝completely incompetent to 100＝competent. Equal distances between stopping points were ten. Reasons of using this scale are similar to the anxiety scale.

(7) Positive expectation of evaluation. Six items of "fear of negative evaluation" were adapted from a brief version of the Fear of Negative Evaluation Scale (FNE) designed by Leary (1983). A five-point scale is changed to six-point scale to form positively-packed ratings (i. e. , 1 = very strongly disagree; 2 = mostly disagree; 3 = slightly agree; 4 = moderately agree; 5 = mostly agree; 6 = strongly agree)(Brown, 2004).

4.4.2 *Documents*

Documents here refer to curriculum related materials like teaching syllabi and textbooks, academic scores, staff information and timetables. It should be cautioned that despite the fact that these ought to be a good source of data, documents are sometimes difficult to obtain because they may be for internal use only or are incomplete and inauthentic (Creswell, 2008). Curriculum materials such as teaching syllabi and textbooks are tools to see whether there are contextual differences between the two groups of BE students (i. e. , high and low WTC) that might have contributed to their varying degrees of WTC.

Two issues were found in the document analysis. A paradox emerged that the teacher in the Teaching Affairs Office mentioned that the university was making efforts to develop the interdisciplinary BE programme rather than BEE and BBE programmes. Thus, the office publicized teaching aims for BEE and BBE students with slight differences on the university's website. Nevertheless, as a matter of fact, teachers and students still kept the idea of distinctions between the BEE and BBE programmes. Also, there were the stated Bachelor of English Education (BEE) programme and scheduled business English related courses for the so-called Bachelor of English (here referred to as BBE) students. In this sense, BEE and BBE will continue to be used in the book.

Another issue is that as only the BE freshmen had the Spoken English course, and it was taught by foreign teachers, for the purpose of obtaining a parallel comparison of BE students' spoken English in different years, the core comprehensive courses of Basic English for freshmen and sophomores, and Senior English for junior students, were chosen to be studied. "Comprehensive" here means that the course is evaluated on the students' four English language skills of reading, writing, speaking and listening. Besides, senior students were busy with internship and had no courses and thus were not included at the time of investigation.

White (1988) presented three major language curriculum value models: the means-ends contextual model (product-aimed), the process model (process-oriented) and the contextual model (school-based and combined process and product orientations) (see Figure 11). According to White, aims and objectives are different in that aims are specific and long-term key objectives while objectives are short or medium-term critical or specific goals. Both aims and objectives are important for a curriculum, because without general aims to guide the direction, a teacher may be lost in carrying out a series of short term objectives (Bell, 1981).

Rational Planners (The means-ends model)
Aims/Purposes→ Objectives→ Learning Experiences→ Evaluation→

Teachers (The process model)
Context→Learning Situation→Aims/Purposes→Evaluation

School-based (The situational model)
Analyze the situation→Define objectives→Design the teaching-learning
programme→Interpret and implement the programme→Assess and evaluate

Figure 11. Three major language curriculum models（White，1988，pp. 33—37）.

Figure 11 shows that the means-ends curriculum model starts from the rational planners' design of aims or purposes to specific or smaller objectives, then to the performances of content and learning experiences according to objectives, and finally to the evaluation of the learning outcome to see if it meets the objectives. The second process model focuses on the procedures rather than the product of the learning. The model is carried out first by teachers' practical concerns about the curriculum context in their workplaces. Then learning contexts such as students' interests and the subjects is considered to form aims or purposes. Evaluation is the final step in the model. However, the process model provides a vague idea of teaching procedures from the aims or purposes to evaluation. The third contextual model combined the means and ends and the process models with an emphasis on both learning process and product. The contextual model is based on the school's analysis of the contextual, then to the definition of objectives, to the design of the teaching programme, to interpret and implement the programme and finally to assess and evaluate the learning outcomes.

In this case, the collected high and low WTC students' curriculum from their teachers were compared for identifying which model teachers used in carrying out the curriculum. Curriculum analysis can help measuring the features of assigned tasks by teachers with regard to duration, interaction and difficulty to students in later classroom observations.

In addition, academic performance is a variable in questionnaires and students' last term's English scores were used. Timetables and staff information were obtained before conducting qualitative studies. It was then possible to make appointments with teachers and students to do interviews and observations.

4.4.3 Student narratives

Each of the selected 12 students was asked to write a narrative. The high and low WTC students were asked to describe their one past and present experience of English classroom learning concerning their WTC. By drawing on a three-dimensional space narrative structure, a researcher is able to retell a personal experience narrative at "interaction (personal and social), continuity (past, present, future) and context (place)" levels (Clandinin & Connelly, 2000, p. 50). However, narratives can be time-consuming and participants find it difficult to suggested usable data (Creswell, 2008). Thus, each student was asked to write only one story and incentives such as money were given to the participants to make them enjoy the writing process.

The collected narratives from high and low WTC BE students were compared. Coffey and Atkinson (1996) suggested the importance of relating content, especially the structure of the narrative with social function in narrative analysis to show the targeted culture. Thus, Labov's (1972) evaluative model for analyzing the structure of narrative was applied, namely: abstract (the topic), orientation (on who, what, when and where), complication (events), evaluation (judge on the events) and resolution (result) and coda (end of the narrative). Students' narratives were re-storied by using the researcher's voice by taking the narrative structure into account.

Prompts were provided to each student participant before they wrote their narratives (see Appendix G). The narrative should include accounts of interactions among teachers and the participant and classmates in past and present English lessons, together with the individual's perceptions of the interactions, WTC in speaking English and reasons for high or low WTC. Narratives were collected in the first interview visit. The collected narratives were then analyzed and grouped into the four WTC categories. Each student's past and present spoken English learning experience was compared and then an evaluation was suggested in each WTC category. Each participant's narrative was translated by the researcher and is reported in the third person. A sample narrative and its translation are provided in Appendix G.

4.4.4 Classroom observations

Non-participant observation was used and field notes were taken in the classrooms. Observational data serves to describe the observed setting, the activities in the setting and the participants in the activities. However, Creswell (2008) argued that disadvantages of observation are: being confined to the accessed sites, difficulty in developing rapport with individuals, and observers' lack of skills to see details and manage issues. The first disadvantage is unavoidable as only a single site case study is investigated. To deal with the second disadvantage, it is essential to make sure that students and teachers are willing to be video-recorded before observation. Considering the last disadvantage, another observer joined in the analysis of observational data with the researcher and inter-rater reliability was assessed.

Planned activities and formal interactions inside the classroom were observed and video-recorded for future reference. Attention was paid to the selected high and low WTC students in each class. Field notes of class observations include the duration of each classroom interaction, the type of an interaction, and a rough estimate of task difficulty (ranging from 1 = extremely easy to 6 = extremely difficult) and how willing the participant seems to communicate (range from 1=strongly unwilling to 6=strongly willing). The criterion to assess task difficulty is according to how linguistically-, cognitively- and affectively-demanding a task is (Gan, 2011). The high-inference observation was later complement by SR data. Interaction in classrooms involves communications between teachers and students as well as communications among students (Alexander, 2000, p. 398). An English teacher from another Chinese university (Jane) and I coded the sheets and inter-rater reliability was calculated. Representative and disagreed video extracts were selected and transcribed. Also, disputed video extracts were discussed to find out why the disagreement was formed. Appendix B shows an observation sheet for one class observation.

4.4.5 Stimulated recalls

In L2 WTC studies, a stimulated recall (SR), be it video or audio-recorded, is used by many researchers (Cao & Philp, 2006; Kang, 2005; MacIntyre, 2007). Generally speaking, though both SR and the "think aloud" method follow the process tracing approach (Ford et al, 1989; Harte et al., 1994; Someren et al., 1994), the strengths of SR lie in its minimal intervention to the research context and its ability to stimulate immediate reflections of the selected context. In contrast, the "think aloud" method requires simultaneous work and reflection in a context, which to some extent hinders reflection. However, reviewing previous studies, Lyle (2003) demonstrated that using video-recorded SR is a problematic method with significant limitations. First, SR retrospective interviews provide incomplete memories and interviewees may react to what they see on the videos rather than recalling the actual episodes themselves. Then, since recalling an event and reflecting on an event are different, additional reflections might emerge out of a researcher's inappropriate probing. In the latter case, I asked participants questions according to the structured SR interview questions. Moreover, one dilemma is to treat a video extract as data or the facilitator of data in SR. In this study, videos were used as a facilitator of data in SR while these video extracts were used as data in analysis of classroom observations.

Since the classroom was large and had many students, classes were video-recorded rather than audio-recorded. Videos here were used as an aid for collecting data rather than as data. Selected extracts from observations serve as the basis for the preceding retrospective interviews. Participants were then asked to reflect on their feelings towards WTC with the playback of videos. In this way, analysis of students' feelings from SR interviews can facilitate the explanation of their actions in observations. At the beginning of an interview, initial verbal cuing, such as research purpose was expressed in order to reduce irrelevant information. After each class, respondents were required to reflect their feelings in the class in response to the replayed videos. Interviews were audio-recorded and then data were transcribed. SR interview questions (referring to Appendix C) were adapted from Cao and Philp (2006) to see participants' WTC in whole class, group and dyadic interactions inside English language classrooms.

4.4.6 Semi-structured interviews

According to Cohen et al. (2000), the research interview serves three purposes. First, it can be regarded as the main method for collecting direct purpose-related information inside a person's mind (Tuckman, 1972). Second, it can be applied to test or propose hypotheses, and third, to explain variables and identify relationships. Results can be linked with other methods to explore unexpected outcomes, to validate other instruments, or to understand better about the motivations of informants, and the reasons they attribute to their ways of responding (Kerlinger, 1970). However, Bell (1999) argued that interviews are not without disadvantages, especially when compared with questionnaires. Though interviews allow more in-depth data collection than questionnaires, they are time-consuming in their administration and analysis. Furthermore, interviewers can be subjective in posing and interpreting interview questions; whereas, questionnaires can appear to be more objective.

Fontana and Frey (1994) suggested that "interviewing has a wide variety of forms and a multiplicity of uses" (p. 361). The main criterion to select the best type of interview for a study is the degree of structure (Kvale, 1996). Cohen et al. (2000) suggested this criterion is connected with the research purpose. The more one wishes to obtain comparable information from different persons and locations, the more structured, standardized and quantitative an interview must be (Harris & Brown, 2010). Conversely, the more one hopes to gain unparalleled, non-standardized, and personalized data, the more unstructured and open-ended an interview tends to be. Besides, in Denscombe's (2003) view, semi-structured interviews enable participants to "develop ideas and speak more widely on the issue raised by the researcher" (p. 167).

Considering the above perspectives, semi-structured individual interviews seem to be suitable in my study. Interview questions with BE students will be designed according to the Chinese WTC model, for the purpose of developing the questionnaire results. With respect to the four categories of factors elaborated by Wen and Clément (2003), interview questions enquire into the participant's perceptions in terms of the four predefined categories: societal context, personality factors, motivational orientation and affective perceptions. In open-ended interview questions (see Appendix D), "what" questions were asked before more probing "why" or "how" questions (Patton, 2002). First, general interview questions about personal information, such as names as well as views about spoken English in terms of DC and WTC were discussed in order to establish rapport between students and researcher. Next, a brief statement of study purpose was essential to be employed as opening declaration (Patton, 2002). Then, the rest of the interview questions were asked. By replaying the audio, interview data with the participants were transcribed. The English teachers were interviewed after interviewing students for the purpose of getting triangulating data from two different perspectives. Interview questions with teachers are listed in Appendix E. All the interviews were audio-recorded and conducted in Chinese. I translated the interview transcripts into English. Then Jane (a local Chinese teacher who was teaching English in another university) helped me checked the accuracy of the translation by listening to the recordings.

To approach verbatim transcription or not is a dilemma for qualitative researchers. There is a move from transcribing the audio recordings word by word to "a process that is sensitive to context, reflexive and constructivist" (Lapadat, 2000, p. 210). Witcher (2010) supported Lapadat's perspective and suggests the quality and trustworthiness of transcription is expressed in how closely the transcript captures the recorded utterances. Also, Poland (1995, 2001) claimed the importance of minimizing not clearly spoken and recorded written text within transcripts. In this study, only words such as "eh""ma""oh" were deleted in the transcripts and clearly intended missing words were added in brackets only when absolutely necessary for readers' comprehension.

4. 5 Data analysis procedures

The project involved data collection through two visits to the case study site. The first visit lasted for two weeks while the second visit lasted a month. At the outset, questionnaires were collected in the first visit. A teacher there helped me distribute the questionnaires to BE students. Participants' responses were entered into an SPSS data file. Academic English scores obtained from the teachers and demographic information was also put into the file. After carrying out questionnaire distribution and statistical analysis, all the qualitative data were collected during the same investigation time and narrative and content analysis were conducted. The documents and student narratives were collected in the second visit. Classroom observation sheets as well as selected transcripts were gathered. All interviews in this research were audio-recorded and then transcribed. The following paragraphs show data analysis steps in this research.

(1) Confirmatory factor analysis (CFA), multi-group CFA, structural equation modeling (SEM) and multi-group SEM of the model were sequentially manipulated in SPSS and Amos to analyze the quantitative data. According to Byrne (2010), SEM takes the confirmatory multivariate approach to analyze a hypothesized structural theory. The features of SEM include that it is confirmatory rather than exploratory and thus it is able to test a pre-specified conceptual model; it is possible to assess measurement errors with the estimates of error variance parameters; and it has not only observed (or manifest) variables but also unobserved (or latent) variables and so on. CFA, as a

member of the SEM family, builds on the researcher's prior knowledge of the latent variable structure. The purpose of conducting CFA is to examine to what extent the observed variables are linked with their latent factors. In this case, CFA was used to evaluate each factor structure based on student responses and structural equation modeling was applied to investigate the effects on variables of WTC and academic performance.

First, data were inspected with regard to normal distribution, missing data and outliers. Next, CFA was conducted. However, since the sample size was small (only 300 in the case study site), multi-group CFA was carried out to examine if there was cross-validity between Pilot Study Two and Study One data for later data combination. If the result comes out to be "configurally non-invariant", it may be that groups vary in their conceptions and thus attach different meanings to the construct (Millsap & Everson, 1991; Millsap & Hartog, 1988; Riordan & Vandenberg, 1994). Then, if CFI difference results in multi-group CFA are smaller than. 001 (indicating invariance), it means there are no differences in the model (Cheung & Rensvold, 2002). Then if CFA outcome shows the items formed the expected scales and multi-group CFA presented cross-validity between Pilot Study Two and Study One data, a structural model can be constructed with combined data drawn from Pilot Study Two and Study One data and SEM will be conducted along with the variables of WTC and academic scores. Finally, multi-group SEM will be applied to investigate if the model and results are equivalent between BEE and BBE students as well as across the different instructors and years.

The reliability and validity of this instrument are worth mentioning. Reliability in quantitative research is "essentially a synonym for consistency and replicability over time, over instruments or over groups of respondents" (Cohen et al., 2000, p. 117). For maintaining good construct reliability, adequate data-model fit (absolute indices, parsimony-adjusted indices and incremental fit indices) and strong factor-variable relationship ($R^2 \geqslant 0.5$) should be obtained (Bandalos & Finney, 2010). Then, if the two requirements are met, external validity can be examined to find if the instrument purportedly measures the Chinese WTC theoretical framework.

(2) Content analysis was used to analyse qualitative data. The qualitative data: documents, classroom observations, narratives, stimulated recalls and semi-structured interviews were analysed thematically with the application of preexisting coding system (Smith, 2000). Considering thematic coding, a table (see Appendix F) was postulated. High and low WTC students were further divided by personal and contextual factors and thus form four situations. The four contexts were then considered as the leading row in the table while the available variables in the Chinese WTC model were viewed as the leading column. The coded qualitative data was then filled in the table.

(3) The last step is to combine quantitative data with qualitative data. Nevertheless, it is not easy to combine quantitative and qualitative data. As mentioned in Section 4.1, Yardley and Bishop (2008) suggested that there may be apparent contradictions between quantitative and qualitative data at the first glance. However, the researcher should try to find the relationships of the two types of data by taking the "context of

each finding" (p. 366) into account. Moreover, these distinct results can suggest new ways for further study.

For linking the results of qualitative and quantitative analysis, the quantifying technique (Tashakkori & Teddlie, 1998) was used by converting qualitative data into quantitative data. According to Sandelowski (2000), qualitative data can first be reduced into items to mean one thing and then be represented numerically. By using the quantifying technique, it is also possible to obtain more information from qualitative data to confirm researchers' assumptions about the data (Sandelowski, 2000). In this case, qualitative data from each instrument in Study Two and Study Three to some extent was first transformed into representative variables and then combined to compare with quantitative data in Study One.

4.6   Ethical issues

Authors report many guidelines to ethical issues in studies (Creswell, 2008; Patton, 2002; Punch, 1998). Mediating their perspectives, the first vital step is not to disclose any information that will harm the participants. Informed consent for accessing to the research setting and the participants were asked. Through e-mails and phone calls, the teachers in the Teaching Affairs Office agreed to help and course teachers and BE students were willing to participate in the study. Then, for protecting the participants, anonymity of the participants has been maintained. In terms of "external audit" (Fraenkel & Wallen, 2006, p. 463), all data elicitation devices such as interview questions were discussed with supervisors. Meanwhile, ensuring the participants knew that they were involved in a research, research purposes (see Section 1. 3) were stated in order to obtain support from them. Moreover, the boundary between me as the investigator and the participants was set up by such as not being a participant observer and confidentiality of data was maintained by no disclosure of information to the employers and/or instructors.

Chapter 5
Pilot Studies

Two pilot studies of translations of the various WTC questionnaire components were undertaken based on Wen and Clément's (2003) Chinese WTC model. The goal of the studies was to ascertain the validity of the translated scales. Presuming the scales were valid, they would be used later in a large-scale study to examine the validity of the WTC model for BE students in Study One. Pilot Study One was used to reduce items in each of the seven WTC factors. After item reduction, the reliability of each factor was tested to be acceptable. Then, Pilot Study Two can be applied to conduct first data screen and then EFA and reliability tests.

5.1 Pilot Study One

As there were too many items in the first draft of the questionnaires, the questionnaires were distributed first for reducing items. A small scale study was applied with 50 participants with equal number of students from BEE and BBE students. Measured variables were WTC, DC, personality, affiliation, anxiety, perceived communication competence and positive expectation of evaluation. The variables were selected based on the factors of WTC, DC, societal factors (group cohesiveness & teacher support), personality (risk-taking & tolerance of ambiguity), motivation (affiliation & task-orientation), attitudes (inhibited monitor & positive expectation of evaluation) in Wen and Clément's (2003) Chinese WTC model (see Figure 3). As mentioned in Section 3.4.1, group cohesiveness and affiliation are interrelated; teacher support is linked with positive expectation of evaluation; task-orientation can be manifested through anxiety and perceived communication competence; inhibited monitor can be expressed through perceived communication competence.

Scales, despite the WTC questionnaire, were revised to include a maximum of six items with the highest standard deviations according to the pilot outcome. Then, the revised questionnaires were tested again with the same number of students. Table 4 shows the reliability coefficients of the seven variables in the first pilot study. It is clear that all the seven variables are acceptable with $\alpha > 0.7$.

Table 4

Reliability coefficients of WTC scales by pilot studies

Scales	Number of items	Cronbach's Alpha	
		Pilot Study One ($N=50$)	Pilot Study Two ($N=295$)
WTC	10	0.93	0.96
DC	6 (pilot one)/ 4 (pilot two)	0.79	0.7
Personality	6	0.78	0.89
Affiliation	5	0.73	0.85

Continued

Scales	Number of items	Cronbach's Alpha	
		Pilot Study One (N=50)	Pilot Study Two (N=295)
Anxiety	6	0.86	0.98
Perceived communication competence	6	0.86	0.96
Positive expectation of evaluation	6	0.72	0.92

5.2   Pilot Study Two

Another pilot study was conducted by using SPSS 16.0 with 299 BE students (of 130 BEE students and 169 BBE students). Exploratory factor analysis (EFA) was applied to examine how well various items are linked with one another and form the factors. Before conducting EFA, data were screened to identify missing data, normality and outliers. The dataset was first checked to see if there was a mistake in data entry.

5.2.1   Data screen

Data were screened to deal with missing data and normality of data. Missing value analysis showed data were tolerable in that no variables with 5% or more missing values and also no joint patterns were found between scale items and demographic information. If data were MCAR (missing completely at random), missing data could be replaced by EM (expectation-maximization) estimation as this method gave "consistent and unbiased estimates of correlations and covariances" (Hill, 1997, p. 42). By using EM estimation, it was found that Little's MCAR test (Hill, 1997) result was not significant with chi-square$=924.288$, $df=918$, $p=0.436>0.05$, suggesting that data were missing completely at random. Also, descriptive results showed that standard deviations of items with missing data were similar after missing data were replaced by EM estimation. The replaced dataset was normally distributed with skewness and kurtosis within the range of -2 to $+2$.

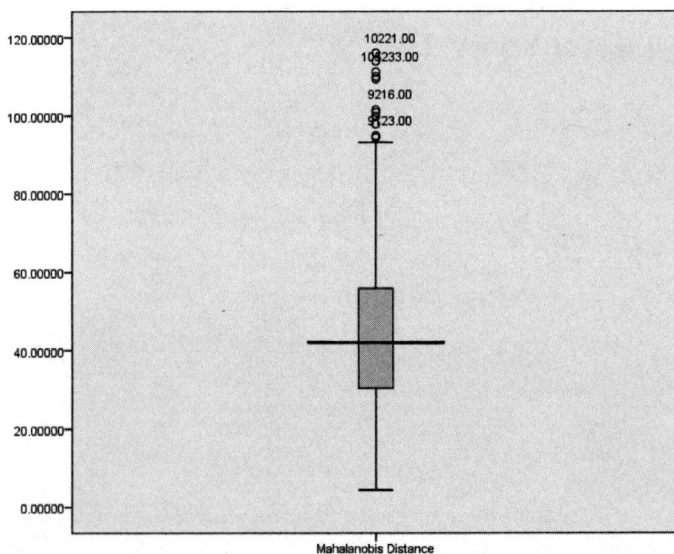

Figure 12. The boxplot of outliers in Pilot Study Two.

The next step of data screen was to remove outliers. For avoiding biased results in exploratory factor analysis, multivariate outliers of Mahalanobis distances were computed. Mahalanobis distances can be used in a large sized dataset to observe how far away outliers are located from the center of the multivariate distribution (Ben-Gal, 2005). The boxplot trimmed four cases out of the dataset (see Figure 12). Outliers were removed from the dataset, resulting in 295 valid cases, of 129 BEE students and 166 BBE students.

5.2.2 Exploratory factor analysis (EFA)

Maximum likelihood (ML) method was then used to explore factors. After applying oblique rotation, the sum of squared structure coefficients of each factor can be seen in Table 5. Seven factors were drawn and in total explained 68.677% of variance. Then, each item's highest factor loading as well as factor correlations were examined.

Table 5

Sums of squared structure coefficients of each factor in Pilot Study Two

Sums of squared structure coefficients of each factor	
Factor 1: Anxiety	22%
Factor 2: Positive Expectation of Evaluation	17%
Factor 3: Perceived Communication Competence	11%
Factor 4: WTC	7%
Factor 5: Personality	5%
Factor 6: Affiliation	4%
Factor 7: DC	2%

The summary of factor loadings and correlations for the WTC questionnaires after item deletion can be seen in Table 6 and factor loadings were acceptable. It was found that all factor loadings were >0.30 but two items originally in the DC scale were removed. One item cross-loaded (crossloadings>0.30) on DC and affiliation and thus was deleted. The last item in DC "I absolutely believe English should be taught at school". was extracted to the affiliation factor. However, theoretically, this item is not about affiliation with a group of people, and thus excluded from the DC scale. In this case, the seven factors drawn were consistent with measured variables. Thus the seven factors were labeled using the names of each scale in Table 5. WTC had the highest factor correlation with a positive expectation of evaluation ($r = 0.47$), indicating the more the students expected positive evaluation from others, the higher WTC they had. For maintaining internal consistency of the questionnaire, the reliability coefficient of each factor was acceptable with $\alpha > 0.7$ (see Table 4).

This chapter outlines two pilot studies of the WTC scales. The two pilot studies turned out to be supportive of Wen and Clément's (2003) Chinese WTC model and suggested the scales of the seven WTC factors found can be applied later in Study One.

Table 6

Summary of factor loadings and correlations for questionnaires
($N = 295$)

Items	Factor loadings						
	1	2	3	4	5	6	7
1. Talk with foreigners about your daily life in English. (BEE)/Have a job interview in English. (BBE)				0.89			

Continued

Items	Factor loadings						
	1	2	3	4	5	6	7
2. Make a speech on a familiar topic in English. (BEE)/ Make or receive a phone call in English. (BBE)				0.79			
3. Read an English article loud and clear in the class. (BEE)/ Make a speech in English. (BBE)				0.78			
4. Talk with native English speakers in English in class. (BEE)/Present in a conference in English. (BBE)				0.92			
5. Read a poem with clear tones and rhymes in English. (BEE)/ Greet someone in English. (BBE)				0.79			
6. Talk with your teacher in English. (BEE)/Organize a meeting in English. (BBE)				0.81			

Continued

Items	Factor loadings						
	1	2	3	4	5	6	7
7. Retell a story in English. (BEE)/Work with your partners in English. (BBE)				0.79			
8. Do a role play in English. (BEE)/Do an oral English translation. (BBE)				0.82			
9. Discuss a topic with your peers in English. (BEE)/Negotiate a business affair in English. (BBE)				0.83			
10. Debate with your peers in English. (BEE)/Talk with an unhappy client in English. (BBE)				0.73			
11. Silent—Talkative					−0.79		
12. Timid—Bold					−0.85		
13. Inactive—Active					−0.90		
14. Inhibited— Spontaneous					−0.80		
15. Unassertive— Assertive					−0.48		

Continued

Items	Factor loadings						
	1	2	3	4	5	6	7
16. Unadventurous— Adventurous					−0.56		
17. When I have assignments to do in English, I try to do them immediately.							0.56
18. I try to read English newspapers or magazines outside my English course work.							0.54
19. I would like the number of English classes at school increased.							0.48
20. I find myself studying English more than other students.							0.52
21. It is effective to study as a group which is composed of people who fit together.						0.82	
22. I enjoy studying with a group which is composed of people who fit together.						0.83	
23. I want to remain a member of a group with which I have worked together previously.						0.37	

Continued

Items	Factor loadings						
	1	2	3	4	5	6	7
24. I come to like the members of a group while interacting with that particular group.						0.63	
25. There is a feeling of unity and cohesion when working as a group which is composed of people who fit together.						0.83	
26. I worry about what other people will think of me even when I know it doesn't make any difference.		0.75					
27. I am frequently afraid of other people noticing my shortcomings.		0.87					
28. I am afraid others will not approve of me.		0.81					
29. I am afraid that people will find fault with me.		0.85					
30. I am usually worried about what kind of impression I make.		0.79					
31. I often worry that I will say or do wrong things.		0.65					

Continued

Items	Factor loadings						
	1	2	3	4	5	6	7
32. Have a small-group conversation in English with acquaintances.	−0.95						
33. Talk in English in a large meeting among friends.	−0.90						
34. Talk in English to friends.	−0.93						
35. Talk in English to acquaintances.	−0.94						
36. Give a presentation in English to a group of acquaintances.	−0.97						
37. Talk in English to a small group of friends.	−0.94						
38. Have a small-group conversation in English with acquaintances.			0.77				
39. Give a presentation in English to a group of friends.			0.86				
40. Have a small-group conversation in English with strangers.			0.81				

Continued

Items	Factor loadings						
	1	2	3	4	5	6	7
41. Talk in English in a large meeting among friends.			0.91				
42. Talk in English in a large meeting with acquaintances.			0.96				
43. Give a presentation in English to a group of acquaintances.			0.91				
Factor correlations							
Factor 1: Anxiety	—						
Factor 2: Positive Expectation of Evaluation	0.14	—					
Factor 3: Perceived Communication Competence	0.21	0.12	—				
Factor 4: WTC	0.016	0.47	0.06	—			
Factor 5: Personality	−0.12	−0.44	−0.20	−0.31	—		
Factor 6: Affiliation	−0.14	−0.22	0.24	−0.30	0.03	—	
Factor 7: DC	0.12	−0.16	0.25	−0.24	0.16	0.27	—

Chapter 6
Study One

This chapter will analyze quantitative findings from Study One, drawing results from Pilot Study Two together. First, how the missing data and outliers in questionnaires were dealt with will be described. Then, CFA and SEM outcomes will be explained. Finally, the findings will be discussed and Research Questions One, Three and Four will be answered. RQ 1 sought to find out personal factors that enable or hinder Chinese BE students' WTC in English classrooms. RQ 3 examined how these factors interacted with each other to influence BE students' WTC. RQ 4 identified pedagogical changes that could contribute to BE students' WTC improvement. These research questions aim to find out the personal factors that assist or hinder BE students'WTC in English language classrooms in China.

6.1 Data screen

Study One was carried out in April, 2011 in Wenzhou University, with 304 BEE and BBE students. The Teaching Affairs Office provided students' academic performance in spoken English (see Section 4.6). Collected spoken English scores and data from questionnaires were first screened for the purpose of obtaining a full dataset without missing data and outliers.

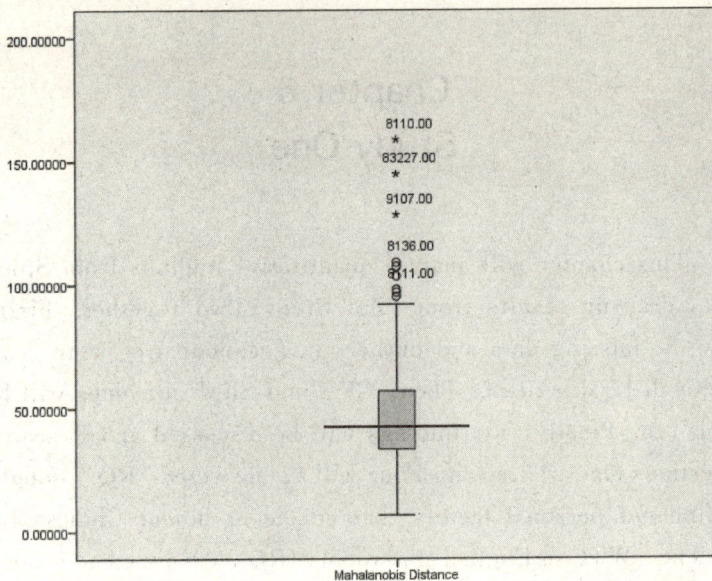

Figure 13. Boxplot of five outliers in Study One.

SPSS 16.0 was used to conduct missing value analysis. If data were MCAR (missing completely at random), missing data could be replaced by EM (expectation-maximization) estimation as this method gives "consistent and unbiased estimates of correlations and covariances" (Hill, 1997, p. 42). Though there were no variables with 5% or more missing values, the tabulated patterns table showed a jointly missing pattern of four cases for DC, positive expectation of evaluation and affiliation variables. One available approach to ML (maximum likelihood) estimation of parameters when data were missing at random was the EM algorithm (Allison, 2003; Enders & Peugh, 2004). By using

EM estimation, Little's MCAR test (Hill, 1997) results were chi-square$=968.847$, $df=842$, $p=0.002<0.05$. Because the significance value was less than 0.05, it was confirmed that data were not missing completely at random. As no variables were found to have more than 10% missing values, it could be inferred that the pattern of missing data was linked only with the observed data, allowing estimates to be adjusted for using existed information, thus data were missing at random (Hill, 1997) and EM estimation of missing values was carried out. Descriptive analysis of variables post MVA showed that standard deviations of items with missing data were similar, since they did not vary much after missing data were replaced by EM estimation. The replaced dataset was normally distributed with skewness within the range of -2 to $+3$ and kurtosis was from -2 to $+4$. Then, multivariate outliers of Mahalanobis distances were computed. The boxplot trimmed 5 cases out of the dataset (see Figure 13). Outliers were removed from the dataset, resulting in 299 valid cases, of 142 BEE students and 157 BBE students.

6.2 Findings

AMOS 18.0 was used to conduct confirmatory factor analysis (CFA) with the pilot study data, multi-group confirmatory factor analysis (MGCFA) of the pilot study and Study One data, structural equation modeling (SEM) with combined pilot study and Study One data as well as multi-group analysis within the SEM (MGSEM) across different instructors, programmes and school years. First, CFA was used to test if the scales can be used to describe the seven WTC factors. Next, for enlarging the database, MGCFA was applied to test if there is cross-validation between Pilot Study Two and Study One. Then, SEM was employed to examine the relation of the WTC inventory and BE students' spoken English scores concerning the model fit indices and standard regression weights. Finally, MGSEM was utilized to do WTC analyses concerning different instructors, programmes and school years to spoken English scores. In addition, in CFA and SEM sections, descriptions of the measurement scale would be presented through SPSS 16. 0.

6. 2. 1 *Confirmatory factor analysis*（*CFA*）

To begin with, using the pilot study data, the seven-factor confirmatory structural model was analyzed. Since it was mentioned in the methodology section that model fit indices were signs of construct reliability（Bandalos & Finney, 2010）, multiple fit indices were used to find the superior model. According to Hooper, Coughlan and Mullen (2008), a range of fit indices, both absolute fit indices, such as chi-square, relative chi-square（$x2/df$）, RMSEA and SRMR, and incremental fit indices. For instance, CFI should be reported in SEM. Absolute fit indices differ from incremental fit indices in that the latter depends on the comparison with a baseline model (Jöreskog & Sörbom, 1993), whereas the former estimates the model fit on the sample data (McDonald & Ho, 2002).

Rather, Fan and Sivo（2007）demonstrate that gamma performs best among a number of fit indices in their models, as it is consistently sensitive to model misspecification, but is generalizable to different types of models or sample sizes.

Absolute indices such as gamma and RMSEA turn out to perform better than incremental fit indices like CFI (Sivo et al. , 2006); however, Fan and Sivo discover that gamma performs even better than RMSEA when the model size is small. While using two smaller models after three designed models and all at two levels and misspecified to the same degrees, it is found that RMSEA is sensitive to the number of variables in a model or to say model size, but gamma is robust to different models. For functional use, gamma equation can be transformed and RMSEA can be inserted into the equation. Interestingly, compared to RMSEA equation, the model size plays an additional important role in the gamma equation. For minimizing the model size effect to the seven-factor 43 items Chinese WTC model in this study, it is important to use gamma along with other fit indices.

In this study, following Peterson, Brown and Irving (2010), chi-square, degree of freedom, x^2/df values (Wheaton et al. , 1977) and p value of x^2/df, goodness of fit indices of CFI (comparative fit index) and gamma (gamma hat) (Fan & Sivo, 2007) as well as badness of fit indices of RMSEA (root-mean-square error of approximation) and SRMR (standard root mean-square residual) were reported. Since chi-square is statistically sensitive to model fit when having a large sample size, practical significance of model fit, for examples, CFI (Bentler, 1990) and RMSEA (Steiger, 1989) should be given in the output. The acceptable rationale of a model is that for x^2/df value is smaller than 5 (Wheaton et al. , 1977) or strictly even 2 (Tabachnick & Fidell, 2007), p is non-significant at 0. 05, CFI and gamma are above or at 0. 90, and RMSEA and SRMR are lower than 0. 08 (Peterson, Brown & Irving, 2010).

Table 7

Confirmatory factor analysis (CFA) results of pilot studies (N= 295)

Model	Items	x^2	df	x^2/df (p)	CFI	gamma	RMSEA	SRMR
CFA Pilot	43	1911.73	839	2.28 (0.13)	0.91	0.85	0.066	0.054
CFA Pilot Modified One	40	1568.44	719	2.18 (0.13)	0.93	0.88	0.063	0.046
CFA Pilot Modified Two	38	2530.74	644	1.97 (0.16)	0.94	0.90	0.058	0.043

Model fit indices of the CFA pilot results (see Table 7) shows that the final version of the second modified model is acceptable with $x^2/df = 1.97$, $p = 0.16$, CFI = 0.94, gamma = 0.90, RMSEA = 0.058 and SRMR = 0.043. The CFA pilot model consists of 43 items in seven WTC factors of WTC, DC, personality, affiliation, anxiety, perceived communication competence and positive expectation of evaluation. The model was modified twice in order to fit the acceptable rationale of a model. Details of model modification will be explained in the following paragraphs.

On the outset, analyzing the seven-factor CFA pilot model with total 43 items obtained from EFA result mentioned in the pilot questionnaires section in the literature review chapter, it can be seen from Table 7 that the model is acceptable with $x^2/df = 2.28$, p value of $x^2/df = 0.13$, CFI = 0.91, RMSEA = 0.066 and SRMR = 0.054; nevertheless, gamma turns out to be 0.85 (smaller than 0.90) for the pilot study model. In order to achieve higher gamma value, three items are taken out of the model for the purpose of modifying the CFA model. According to Bandalos and Finney

(2010), a strong factor-variable relationship ($R^2 \geqslant 0.5$) should be assured to maintain construct reliability. The three deleted items have low standardized regression weights, of smaller than 0.5 to their respective factors, meaning the variance explained of only 0.25. Meanwhile, modification indices show that these items were to some extent attracted to other factors. The three items are: The one with choices can be selected from the dichotomy of unassertive and assertive in the personality factor, the item "I found myself studying English more than the others" in the DC factor and the last item "I want to remain a member of a group with which I have worked together previously" in the affiliation factor.

After item deletion, the model with 40 items run again. Since fit was still below recommended thresholds, the modification indices were inspected. Two more items showed strong factor cross-loadings; one was "I worry about what other people will think of me, even when I know it doesn't make any difference" in the positive expectation of evaluation factor and the other item was "Discuss a topic with your peers in English" for BEE students and "Negotiate a business affair in English" for BBE students in the WTC factor, which was removed from the model. The model after the deletions run again and had sufficiently robust fit statistics and so was accepted as a sufficient representation of the participants' willingness to communicate. Finally, there were in total 38 items drawn in this Chinese WTC model. The final model kept the seven WTC factors of WTC, DC, personality, affiliation, anxiety, perceived communication competence and positive expectation of evaluation, and items in the revised questionnaire which could be seen in Table 3.

6.2.2　*Multi-group confirmatory factor analysis* (*MGCFA*)

The next step was to use multi-group confirmatory factor analysis（MGCFA）to examine if there was cross-validity between the pilot study data and the actual study data（Byrne, 2004）. The two datasets were collected at different times from the same population in the case study site. A problem of using the same participants for the pilot and the main study was that the measured attitudes might be unstable over time（Bertrand & Mullainathan, 2001）. Thus MGCFA was used to examine if the measured attitudes were invariant between the two datasets.

Table 8

Model comparisons for pilot and Study One data

Model	$x^2(\Delta x^2)$	df（Δdf）	p	CFI（ΔCFI）
Unconstrained	2530.74	1288		0.940
Measurement weights	（34.40）	（31）	0.31	（0.001）
Structural covariances	（189.26）	（28）	0.00	（0.006）
Measurement residuals	（108.28）	（38）	0.00	（0.003）

Note：Δ＝change in statistics.

MGCFA was computer generated model comparisons of the pilot and the main study to ensure that the model parameters were invariant across the two samples. The baseline model is unconstrained. Measurement weights model refers to invariant factor loadings while structural covariances model points to invariant covariances between factors. Measurement residuals model is the strictest model implying that unexplained residuals for each item are equivalent. The changes in statistics were calculated on the basis of nested comparisons (Wu, 2009), that is, comparing measurement weights model with the unconstrained model, then structural covariances model with the measurement weights model, and eventually measurement residuals model with the structural covariances model.

The multi-group confirmatory factor analysis results (see Table 8) show that the models are equivalent. RMSEA $= 0.040$ in the unconstrained model demonstrated that the construct was configurally invariant (Buss & Royce, 1975; Irvine, 1969; Peterson, Brown & Irving, 2010; Suzuki & Rancer, 1994). The existence of configural invariance means that different groups have the same number of factors and associated items as well as identical paths among and between factors and items (Meredith, 1993). Table 8 shows that changes of CFI were smaller than 0.01, indicating invariance (Cheung & Rensvold, 2002). Also, in the measurement weights model $p = 0.31$, meaning statistically non-significant and showing invariance. That implies that differences between the models are within chance, as the parameters are equivalent for the two models. Thus, findings of multi-group confirmatory factor analysis point out that the factorial structure of the pilot study can be cross-validated on Study one. Since pilot study and Study One data are collected from the same population, it is possible to combine data from the two studies to form a larger dataset to conduct SEM.

It would also be essential to describe elements concerning the measurement scale, namely reliability coefficients, factor loadings, means and standard deviations of the factors and items in Study One (see Table 9). Table 3 shows that the reliability coefficients and item loadings on each factor are acceptable. Among the seven factors, DC has the lowest reliability coefficients ($\alpha=0.68$). The other six factors' coefficient alphas are much higher, ranging from 0.88 to 0.98. However, while applying Cronbach's alpha as a reliability estimate, the value obtained is not consistent with the test score's reliability, according to inter-item covariances and measurement errors. Sijtsma (2009) proposed the use of greatest lower bound (glb) reliability to accompany the report of alpha. For the whole WTC questionnaire, the reliability coefficients were acceptable with $\alpha=0.819$, glb = 0.986 ($k>3$) in EQS 6. All the items have loadings higher than 0.5, and load on the conceptually-expected factor. Searching through the composite mean scores for the seven variables, it can be inferred that BE students were low in anxiety (30.05/1.80 at a six point range), but moderate in the other six factors of WTC (3.9), positive expectation of evaluation (4.02), perceived communication competence (58.05/3.48 at a six point range), personality (5.44/4.66 at a six point range), DC (4.26) and affiliation (4.75).

Table 9

Descriptions of the measurement scale in Study One ($N=299$)

Factors and items $\alpha=0.819$, glb=0.986 ($k>3$)	M	SD	λ
WTC (9 items, six-point scale) $\alpha=0.95$	3.9	1.07	
Talk with foreigners about your daily life in English. (BEE)/ Have a job interview in English. (BBE)	4.11 3.74	1.33	0.829

Continued

Factors and items $\alpha=0.819$, glb$=0.986$ (k$>$3)	M	SD	λ
Make a speech on a familiar topic in English. (BEE)/ Make or receive a phone call in English. (BBE)	3.79 3.86	1.24	0.846
Read an English article loud and clear in the class. (BEE)/ Make a speech in English. (BBE)	4.30 3.80	1.26	0.854
Talk with native English speakers in English in class. (BEE)/ Present in a conference in English. (BBE)	4.22 3.76	1.26	0.826
Read a poem with clear tones and rhymes in English. (BEE)/ Greet someone in English. (BBE)	3.96 3.98	1.26	0.829
Talk with your teacher in English. (BEE)/ Organize a meeting in English. (BBE)	4.15 3.70	1.27	0.860
Retell a story in English. (BEE)/ Work with your partners in English. (BBE)	3.93 3.85	1.24	0.807
Do a role play in English. (BEE)/ Do an oral English translation. (BBE)	4.27 3.62	1.28	0.775
Debate with your peers in English. (BEE)/ Talk with an unhappy client in English. (BBE)	3.77 3.59	1.25	0.809
Anxiety (6 items, 0—100 scale with 10 as intervals) $\alpha=0.98$	30.05	25.05	
Have a small-group conversation in English with acquaintances.	27.96	27.54	0.925
Talk in English in a large meeting among friends.	32.71	25.36	0.909

Continued

Factors and items α＝0.819，glb＝0.986 (k＞3)	M	SD	λ
Talk in English to friends.	28.13	27.56	0.929
Talk in English to acquaintances.	31.88	26.37	0.947
Give a presentation in English to a group of acquaintances.	29.19	25.77	0.962
Talk in English to a small group of friends.	30.44	26.40	0.929
Positive expectation of evaluation（5 items，six-point scale，reverse coded）α＝0.88	4.02	0.87	
I am frequently afraid of other people noticing my shortcomings.	4.06	1.07	0.754
I am afraid others will not approve of me.	3.94	1.05	0.756
I am afraid that people will find fault with me.	3.96	1.05	0.825
I am usually worried about what kind of impression I make.	4.06	1.03	0.797
I often worry that I will say or do wrong things.	4.07	1.07	0.745
Perceived communication competence（6 items，0—100 scale with 10 as interval）α＝0.96	58.05	19.31	
Have a small-group conversation in English with acquaintances.	62.16	21.31	0.829
Give a presentation in English to a group of friends.	59.93	21.44	0.878
Have a small-group conversation in English with strangers.	55.18	20.96	0.877
Talk in English in a large meeting among friends.	53.44	21.39	0.910

Continued

Factors and items α＝0. 819, glb＝0. 986 (k＞3)	M	SD	λ
Talk in English in a large meeting with acquaintances.	56. 25	21. 46	0. 944
Give a presentation in English to a group of acquaintances.	61. 30	20. 84	0. 895
Personality (5 items, nine-point scale) α＝0. 91	5. 44	1. 45	
Silent→ Talkative	5. 46	1. 81	0. 888
Timid→Bold	5. 50	1. 65	0. 802
Inactive→Active	5. 50	1. 70	0. 913
Inhibited→Spontaneous	5. 57	1. 69	0. 869
Unadventurous→Adventurous	5. 19	1. 64	0. 584
DC (3 items, six-point scale) α＝0. 68	4. 26	0. 84	
When I have assignments to do in English, I try to do them immediately.	4. 56	1. 05	0. 667
I try to read English newspapers or magazines outside my English course work.	4. 28	1. 05	0. 694
I would like the number of English classes at school increased.	3. 95	1. 15	0. 567
Affiliation (4 items, six-point scale) α＝0. 88	4. 75	0. 82	
It is effective to study as a group which is composed of people who fit together.	4. 71	1. 03	0. 839
I enjoy studying with a group which is composed of people who fit together.	4. 79	0. 98	0. 879
I come to like the members of a group while interacting with that particular group.	4. 60	0. 89	0. 703

			Continued
Factors and items α＝0. 819，glb＝0. 986 (k＞3)	M	SD	λ
There is a feeling of unity and cohesion when working as a group which is composed of people who fit together.	4. 88	0. 94	0. 769

Note：λ＝loadings as standardized beta regressions.

6.2.3　*Structural equation modeling（SEM）*

While CFA draws the measurement model of the Chinese WTC model，SEM can combine the CFA measurement model into a structural model to perform simultaneous multivariate analysis（Hoe，2008）. The structural model is presented in Figure 14. The figure was made up of total eight variables of the seven inter-correlated latent variables of WTC，DC，personality，affiliation，anxiety，perceived communication competence and positive expectation of evaluation to predict an observed variable of students' speaking scores.

It is important to decide the minimum sample size required before data collection for the purpose of reaching the desired statistical power（McQuitty，2004）. Although researchers diverge in their opinions about the sample size for SEM（Sivo et al.，2006），the generally accepted value is ten participants per free parameter estimated（Schreiber et al.，2006）. In this structural model，there are 105 free parameters，thus the sample size should be 1050；however，there were not enough participants in the case study size. According to Hoe（2008），Garver and Mentzer（1999）and Hoelter（1983），the critical sample size in SEM can be 200. In light of these points，as there

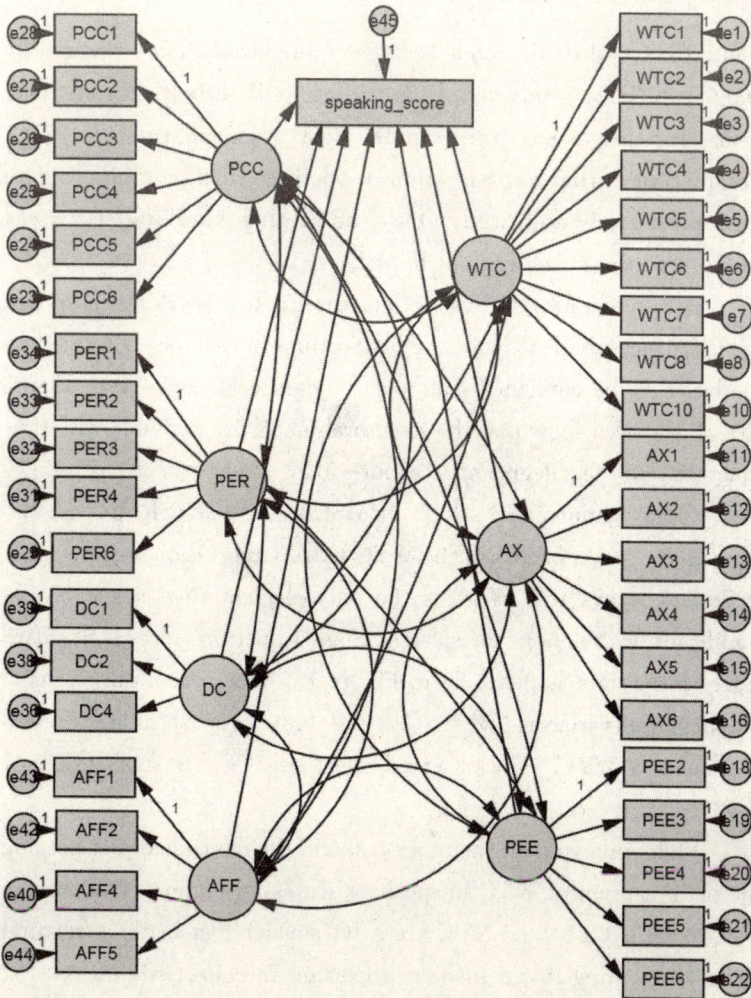

Figure 14. Structural model of the CFA measurement incorporating speaking scores.

Note: WTC=willingness to communicate, AX=anxiety, PEE=positive expectation of evaluation, PCC=perceived communication competence, PER=personality, DC=desire to communicate with a specific person，AFF＝affiliation.

was cross-validity detected between pilot study data and Study One data，pilot study data were integrated into the Study One data. In this case，the sample size was enlarged to 594. Conducting structural equation modeling with combined data from pilot study and Study One，the English speaking score was added into the measurement model.

After integrating the variable of the English speaking score into the CFA measurement model，the structural model was calculated on the basis of the combined data and standard coefficients（see Figure 15）. Fit indices show that the structural model is acceptable with Chi-square＝1608. 84，degree of freedom＝675，x^2/df＝2. 38，p＝0. 12，CFI＝0. 96，gamma hat＝0. 93，RMSEA＝0. 048，SRMR＝0. 03. Among the seven factors in the WTC model，regression weights table in Scalars shows that WTC is the only element that is statistically significant in relation to spoken English performances. Standard regression weight is β＝0. 22 in Figure 15，that means only a small proportion of variance（R^2＝5％，f^2＝0. 053）in speaking score is explained by WTC. The observed effect size（f^2）is small（Cohen，1992）.

While removing all the other paths in the model and just keeping the path diagram of WTC to speaking scores，the standard regression weights（β＝0. 21）and SMC are a bit smaller that in the structural model，indicating that a smaller proportion and effect size（R^2＝4％，f^2＝0. 042）of speaking score is explained by WTC. Thus，the path diagram suggests speaking scores is not solely affected by WTC and there are other influential factors as the SEM model suggested.

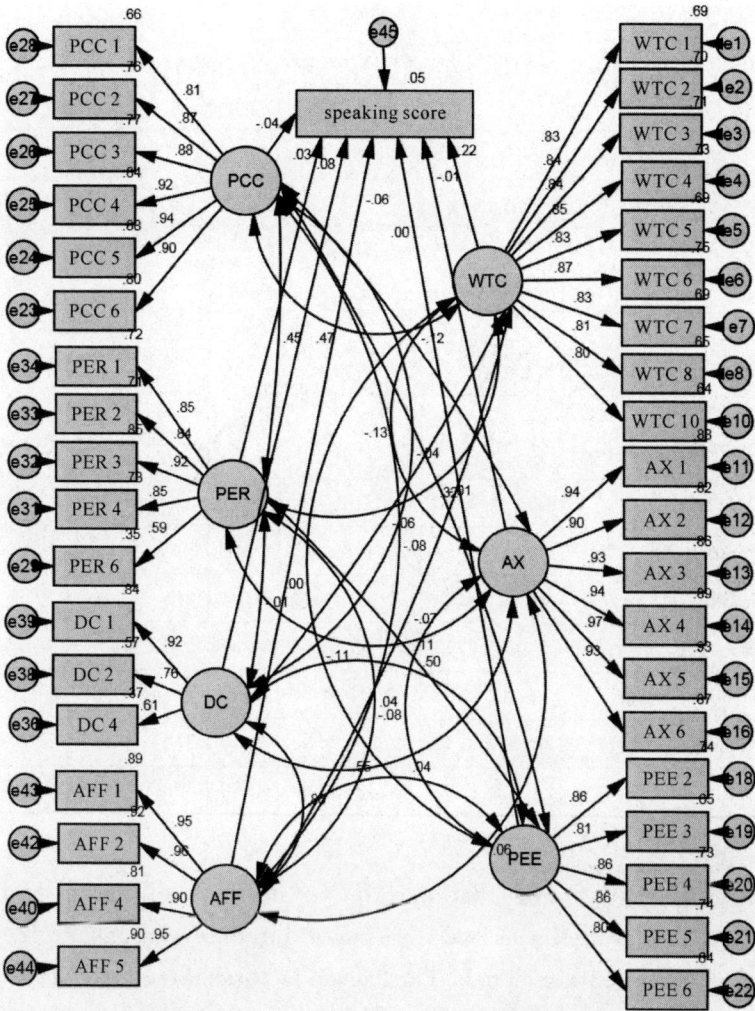

Figure 15. Standardized coefficients for SEM.

Table 10

Descriptive statistics and factor inter-correlations in SEM（N=594）

Chinese WTC factors	Inter-correlations							
	1	2	3	4	5	6	7	8
Anxiety	—							
Positive expectation of evaluation	−0.08	—						
Perceived Communication competence	−0.12	−0.01	—					
WTC	−0.13	0.00	**0.47**	—				
Personality	−0.11	0.11	0.45	**0.32**	—			
Affiliation	0.06	0.55	−0.08	−0.07	0.04	—		
DC	0.04	0.50	−0.05	−0.06	−0.02	**0.86**	—	
Speaking score	−0.01	0.00	−0.04	0.22	0.03	−0.06	0.08	—
M	28.54	3.49	59.59	3.99	5.42	3.41	3.47	79.85
SD	24.78	1.03	18.83	1.08	1.50	1.56	1.16	7.01

Note: Numbers in bold are mentioned in the paragraph.

Table 10 shows that descriptive statistics of means and standard deviations as well as factor inter-correlations in the structural equation model. The "seven factors" inter-correlations in the Chinese WTC structural model are mostly from moderate to low, with the high correlation between DC factor and affiliation factor ($r=0.86$, $r^2=0.74$) as an exception. WTC has positive correlations with perceived communication competence ($r=0.47$) and personality ($r=0.32$). In addition, mean scores show low anxiety and moderate levels in the other six variables.

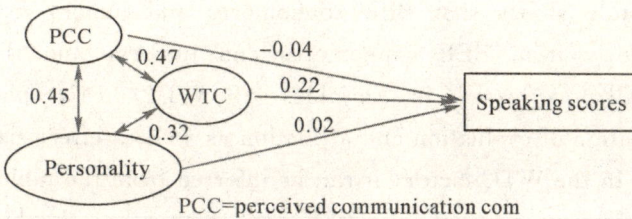

PCC=perceived communication com

Figure 16. Path diagram of WTC, PCC and personality to speaking score.

Note: PCC=perceived communication competence.

Figure 16 models a diagram including paths of WTC, perceived communication competence and personality to speaking scores. WTC explained most speaking scores and the variance explained was similar to that in the structural model; however, variance explained by personality and perceived communication competence to speaking scores was quite small. WTC ($\beta = 0.22$, $R^2 = 5\%$) and personality ($\beta = 0.02$, $R^2 = 0.04\%$) were found to be positively related with speaking scores whereas perceived communication competence ($\beta = -0.04$, $R^2 = 0.16\%$) was negatively related with speaking scores. The figure then indicates perceived communication competence and personality were indirectly related to speaking scores through WTC. The variance explained between perceived communication competence and WTC ($\beta = 0.47$, $R^2 = 22\%$), between personality and WTC ($\beta = 0.32$, $R^2 = 10\%$) as well as between perceived communication competence and personality ($\beta = 0.45$, $R^2 = 20\%$) were positive.

6.2.4 *Multi-group structural equation modeling* (*MGSEM*)

Table 11 shows the effect on oral English scores of different instructors and programmes. Standard regression weights, effect sizes of SMC and student numbers were included in the table. The table shows that BBE sophomores and juniors respond differently from BEE sophomores and juniors, and this is especially expressed in variables of WTC, DC, positive expectation of evaluation and affiliation as well as effect sizes of SMC. In the WTC factor, it can be inferred from the table that T2, who was teaching the BEE sophomores has the highest standard regression weight of 0.47.

However, while T6 has $\beta = 0.28$, T5 has a contrary score -0.28. Also, BEE students ($\beta = 0.35$) can explain much more of the total variance ($\beta = 0.22$) than BBE students ($\beta = 0.07$). In DC, the standard regression weights in T5 ($\beta = 0.42$) and T6 ($\beta = 0.57$) are far higher than those in other teachers. BBE students ($\beta = 0.27$) account for DC's standard regression weights of 0.08, whereas BEE students have only $\beta = -0.05$. In anxiety factor, T5 has the highest standard regression weight of 0.23. Other data in this factor are much smaller. In positive expectation of evaluation, T2 ($\beta = 0.31$) and T3 ($\beta = -0.24$) perform differently from T5 to T6. In affiliation, T5 ($\beta = -0.80$) and T6 (-0.46) distinct greatly from T2 to T3, meaning that BE students cannot get a feeling of togetherness while conducting group work conducted by their teachers. BBE students have negative low standard regression weight of -0.20 than BEE students ($\beta = 0.10$). No obvious distinctions are shown in the personality factor. In perceived communication competence, T1 has the highest standard regression weight of 0.23. Regarding the effect size of SMC, except T2 (0.25) and T5 (0.23), who have medium effect size, other data are small. The difference between the BEE and BBE sophomores and juniors suggests it may be that students enrolled in BEE and BBE programmes are different or their teachers carried out spoken English classes in different ways.

Table 11

Effect on oral English score by different instructors and programmes

	Effect on oral English score								
	T1	T2	T3	T4	T5	T6	BEE	BBE	Total
WTC	0. 11	0. 47	0. 02	0. 14	−0. 28	**0. 28**	**0. 35**	**0. 07**	0. 22
DC	−0. 06	−0. 19	0. 04	−0. 19	**0. 42**	**0. 57**	−**0. 05**	**0. 27**	0. 08
Anxiety	0. 01	0. 08	−0. 19	0. 00	**0. 23**	0. 00	−0. 06	0. 07	−0. 01
Positive expectation of evaluation	−0. 07	**0. 31**	−**0. 24**	0. 04	0. 07	−0. 12	0. 01	−0. 04	0. 00
Affiliation	0. 02	0. 01	0. 17	0. 24	−**0. 80**	−**0. 46**	**0. 10**	−**0. 20**	−0. 06
personality	−0. 13	−0. 17	0. 07	0. 09	−0. 16	0. 06	−0. 06	0. 10	0. 03
Perceived communication competence	**0. 23**	−0. 21	0. 19	0. 06	0. 16	−0. 21	−0. 07	0. 01	−0. 04
Effect SMC	0. 05	**0. 25**	0. 14	0. 07	**0. 23**	0. 09	0. 11	0. 04	0. 05
Student number	98	100	70	112	79	135	271	323	594
Grade	1	2	3	1	2	3			
Programme	BEE	BEE	BEE	BBE	BBE	BBE			

Note: T=teacher. Numbers in bold are mentioned in the paragraph.

A computation was done to see if learning experience can make a change to BE students' WTC. Merging the sophomores and juniors into a group and the freshmen into another group respectively for BEE and BBE programmes, an independent samples T-test examined whether the differences between the mean scores of two groups were significant for the two programmes. Table 12 shows the BEE freshmen were higher than the BEE sophomores and juniors in WTC ($M=4.62$, $SD=0.89$ versus $M=3.75$, $SD=1.09$, $t(235.70)=7.13$, $p=0.000$), personality ($M=5.58$, $SD=1.56$ versus $M=5.16$, $SD=1.56$, $t(266)=2.13$, $p=0.034$) and perceived communication competence ($M=66.40$, $SD=18.20$ versus $M=56.01$, $SD=19.31$, $t(266)=4.33$, $p=0.000$).

Also, BBE freshmen were higher than BBE sophomores and juniors in WTC ($M=4.21$, $SD=1.04$ versus $M=3.77$, $SD=1.02$, $t(324)=3.69$, $p=0.000$), DC ($M=3.70$, $SD=1.26$ versus $M=3.33$, $SD=0.99$, $t(185.05)=2.66$, $p=0.009$), affiliation ($M=3.62$, $SD=1.58$ versus $M=3.10$, $SD=1.48$, $t(324)=2.94$, $p=0.003$) and positive expectation of evaluation ($M=3.73$, $SD=1.03$ versus $M=3.31$, $SD=0.97$, $t(324)=3.68$, $p=0.000$). That is, compared with BE freshmen, BEE sophomores' and juniors' WTC, the level of extrovert personality and perceived communication competence decreased while BBE sophomores' and juniors' WTC, DC, affiliation and positive expectation of evaluation lowered.

Table 12

T-test scores for year one and years two and three groups

	Group	N	M	SD	t	df	sig. (2-tailed)
WTC	1	98	4. 62	0. 89			
	2	170	3. 75	1. 09	7. 13	235. 70	0. 00 *
	3	112	4. 21	1. 04	3. 69	324. 00	0. 00 *
	4	214	3. 77	1. 02			
DC	1	98	3. 53	1. 30	0. 38	266. 00	0. 71
	2	170	3. 47	1. 18			
	3	112	3. 70	1. 26			
	4	214	3. 33	0. 99	2. 66	185. 05	0. 01 *
Anxiety	1	98	25. 26	28. 24	−1. 63	266. 00	0. 10
	2	170	30. 53	23. 72			
	3	112	26. 77	24. 35	−0. 92	324. 00	0. 36
	4	214	29. 38	24. 09			
Positive Expectation of Evaluation	1	98	3. 67	1. 07	1. 58	266. 00	0. 12
	2	170	3. 46	1. 04			
	3	112	3. 73	1. 03	3. 68	324. 00	0. 00 *
	4	214	3. 31	0. 97			
Affiliation	1	98	3. 69	1. 79			
	2	170	3. 50	1. 43	0. 88	168. 61	0. 38
	3	112	3. 62	1. 58	2. 95	324. 00	0. 00 *
	4	214	3. 10	1. 48			

Continued

	Group	N	M	SD	t	df	sig. (2-tailed)
Personality	1	98	5.58	1.56	2.13	266.00	0.03 *
	2	170	5.16	1.56			
	3	112	5.47	1.49	−0.30	324.00	0.77
	4	214	5.52	1.42			
Perceived Communication Competence	1	98	66.40	18.20	4.33	266.00	0.00 *
	2	170	56.01	19.31			
	3	112	57.42	19.04	−1.43	324.00	0.16
	4	214	60.45	17.81			

Note: * the mean difference is significant at the .05 level.

　　1＝BEE freshmen, 2＝BEE sophomores, 3＝BBE juniors, 4＝BBE seniors.

Table 13

Model comparisons across different instructors, programmes and years

	Model	x^2 (Δx^2)	df (Δdf)	p	CFI (ΔCFI)
Instructors	Unconstrained	6574.32	4050		0.90
	Measurement weights	(270.55)	(190)	0.00	(0.00)
	Structural covariances	(216.39)	(140)	0.00	(0.00)
	Measurement residuals	(723.80)	(195)	0.00	(0.02)
Programmes	Measurement weights	(67.83)	(38)	0.00	(0.00)
	Structural covariances	(24.46)	(28)	0.02	(0.00)
	Measurement residuals	(240.27)	(39)	0.00	(0.01)
	Unconstrained	2543.41	1350		0.95

Continued

	Model	x^2 (Δx^2)	df (Δdf)	p	CFI (ΔCFI)
	Unconstrained	3486. 94	2025		0. 94
Years	Measurement weights	(97. 67)	(76)	0. 05	(0. 00)
	Structural covariances	(110. 41)	(56)	0. 00	(0. 00)
	Measurement residuals	(226. 74)	(78)	0. 00	(0. 01)

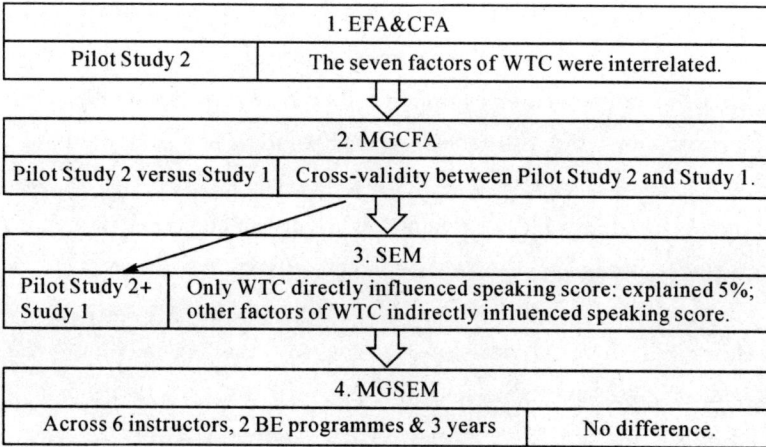

1. EFA&CFA	
Pilot Study 2	The seven factors of WTC were interrelated.

$\Downarrow$

2. MGCFA	
Pilot Study 2 versus Study 1	Cross-validity between Pilot Study 2 and Study 1.

$\Downarrow$

3. SEM	
Pilot Study 2+ Study 1	Only WTC directly influenced speaking score: explained 5%; other factors of WTC indirectly influenced speaking score.

$\Downarrow$

4. MGSEM	
Across 6 instructors, 2 BE programmes & 3 years	No difference.

Figure 17. Main findings of the survey.

It seems there are some effect differences among BE students but the equivalence test reveals the apparent differences are statistically random differences. Multi-group analysis of the structural model across different instructors, programmes and years is carried out with one comparison at one time. RMSEA values for the six instructors (0. 033), the two English programmes (0. 039) and the three years (0. 035) in the unconstrained models are all lower than 0. 05, indicating configural invariance. Table 13 shows that although most changes of CFI are smaller than 0.01, indicating invariance. That implies different English instructors, programmes and school years tends to be unvaried as to the structural model. However, CFI indices shows that the model comparison across different instructors (0.90) is fitting less well than for programmes (0.95) and years (0.94).

6.3   Discussion

Figure 17 shows the main findings of the survey. In the first step, EFA was used to establish a link between the items on the questionnaires and the factors identified by Wen and Clément. Items that could not be linked were discarded. In this case, two items were discarded. Linkages were established between the remaining items and the seven factors. Then, CFA was used to validate the factors on the scale. In other words, this procedure confirmed the relationships between the items on the questionnaires and the factors, as well as the relationships among the factors. Five items were deleted in CFA. In statistical terms, EFA was conducted for linking significant items to its factors while CFA was used to validate the scale developed from EFA. The outcome showed that the seven factors of DC, WTC, personality, affiliation, anxiety, perceived communication competence and positive expectation of evaluation were interrelated with each other in the CFA model.

In the second step, MGCFA was used to validate the linkages between the items and the factors as well as among the factors for two groups: the pilot and the main study. The purpose of this step was to compare the linkages for the two groups. In statistical terms, multi-group CFA was used to see if there was cross-validity between the pilot study data and the actual study data. The finding showed that. Thus it was able to combine the pilot study data and the actual study data to form a larger database for SEM.

In the third step, SEM was used to examine the relationships between the items on the questionnaires and the factors, as well as the relationships among the seven factors and speaking scores. In statistical terms, adding spoken English scores into the CFA model, the structural equation model showed that only a small proportion of variance of only 5% in speaking scores was explained by WTC. Variance was the standard deviation (dispersion of any set of numerical values about mean) squared. In this study, WTC was the independent variable and speaking score was the dependent variable. A set of WTC scores predicted 5% standard deviation squared of a set of speaking scores. This result showed that WTC indeed could influence students' speaking score, though the influence was not very strong. It indicated that the other six factors of WTC indirectly influenced speaking scores through WTC. It also suggested that there were strong direct influence of other factors on students' speaking scores and future research could explore these factors.

In the last step, MGSEM was used to compare the relationships between the items on the questionnaires and the factors, as well as the relationships among the seven factors and speaking scores for different groups. In statistical terms, multi-group SEM was then conducted with six instructors, two English programmes and three years separately. It was found that there was no difference between the six instructors, two English programmes and three years.

The findings of Study One mentioned above proved the existence of a small but statistically significant relationship between Bachelor of English students' WTC and their spoken English performances in the English language classroom; however, other factors in the seven-factor Chinese WTC model were found to be indirectly associated with students' academic scores regarding spoken English. The three research questions for searching the personal factors that influenced Chinese BE students' WTC can be answered to some extent. Research Questions One "what personal factors hinder and enable individual BE students' spoken English in English classrooms" and Three "how do these factors interact to influence WTC in English language classrooms" were uncovered first. To begin with, the WTC model was modified to meet the acceptable rationale of a model. Next, through CFA and multi-group CFA results, this study confirmed reliability and validity of the seven-factor Chinese WTC measurement model. Then, adding spoken English scores into the CFA measurement model to form a SEM, revealed that only one of the seven factors, WTC, explained roughly 5% of the spoken English scores and the other factors in the measurement model had no relation to the academic performance in speaking. Finally, multi-group SEM results suggested that different instructors, BE programmes and students in different years were unvaried as to the structural model. Research Question Four about pedagogical changes to enhance BE students' WTC in English classrooms was then suggested based on findings drawn from Research Questions One and Three.

6.3.1 Research Questions One—personal factors that facilitate or hinder BE students' WTC, and Three—interactions between personal and contextual factors

The study showed BE students are somewhat willing to communicate in English classrooms. Low anxiety can assist students' spoken English study inside classrooms; nevertheless, the other six factors of WTC, DC, positive expectation of evaluation, affiliation, personality and perceived communication competence in the seven factors Chinese WTC model were found to be at moderate levels, meaning students need to face the hindrances caused by these factors. Next, as to RQ 3, the Chinese WTC model shows that the seven factors are inter-correlated, suggesting all the seven factors intertwine with each other to influence BE students' WTC.

At the outset, the seven-factor WTC model was modified twice and the final model was drawn up by first deleting three items and then removing two items. These five items in the WTC model were found to be attracted to other factors. For instance, the covariances and regression weights tables show the error value of the item needed to be deleted from the positive expectation of evaluation factor was attached to the affiliation factor. However, theoretically, the meaning of this item is different from affiliation. Affiliation is about the sense of togetherness within a group. But this item is concerned with the effect of others' impression on a respondent. Meanwhile, the covariances table suggests that the mentioned item in WTC factor is linked with the other four items' error values in the WTC factor to some strength and is also removed from the model. One assumption attributing to the removal of these items may be caused by the different sample size, of only 50 in Pilot Study One and of 295 in Pilot Study Two. The sample size in Pilot Study One may be too small to represent the whole BE population.

Secondly, the seven-factor Chinese WTC model built in this study confirms the Chinese conceptualization of WTC suggested by Wen and Clément (2003). The seven variables in the Chinese WTC model of WTC, DC, anxiety, positive expectation of evaluation, affiliation, personality and perceived communication competence are inter-correlated with each other. It implies the DC and the four factors in Wen and Clément's (2003) model, of "societal context (group cohesiveness & teacher support), personality factors (risk-taking & tolerance of ambiguity), motivational orientations (affiliation & task-orientation) and affective perceptions (inhibited monitor & positive expectation of evaluation)" (p. 25) were inter-linked with each other to influence WTC.

The mean scores of the factors in CFA and SEM shows that BE students have low anxiety, but possess moderate levels in the other six variables. Adjusting the means scores in the same six point scale, anxiety was just 1.8, indicating the respondents were mostly relaxed whereas the other six variables were between 3.48 and 4.75, indicating a range between slightly agree to moderately agree. The discovery of students' low anxiety to speak English in English classrooms challenges the stereotyped view of Chinese students at the cultural level in English language learning in China, and is in line with findings by Garrott (1995) and Shi (2006) as mentioned in Section 3.4.2, concerning some

Chinese learners of English's move of collectivism to individualism under the influence of globalization.

However, this outcome partially contradicts Wen and Clément's Chinese conceptualization of WTC with regard to the assumption that the Chinese students are anxious in English classrooms. As Wen and Clément claim, Chinese students with the universal DC may have low WTC because of the hindrances from the other five factors in the WTC model, which is not the case in this study as respondents report they are relatively relaxed while facing different proposed situations in English language classes.

Thirdly, according to the inter-factor correlations in SEM section, DC and affiliation are strongly connected and explained 74% of variance. Meanwhile, the mean score of affiliation was the highest among the seven WTC factors in the model, of 4.75, suggesting that the students tend to be affiliated to others in English classrooms most of the time. From my past teaching experience, the reason may be that undergraduate students are required to live on campus, and thus they have a close relationship with a certain group of friends, especially roommates, with whom they sit and study together. These close friends or roommates can to some extent stimulate their desire to communicate in classroom interactions such as group work while forming the feeling of togetherness with the group members.

Nonetheless, WTC turns out to be only correlated with perceived communication competence and personality. Along with the development of WTC theories in the second language learning, perceived communication competence and personality have long been associated with WTC by many scholars in this field mentioned in the literature review (Cao & Philp, 2006; de Saint Léger & Storch, 2009; Fushino, 2010; Kang, 2005; MacIntyre et al. , 2001; MacIntyre, Burns & Jessome, 2011; MacIntyre & Legatto, 2011). By modeling paths of WTC, perceived communication competence and personality to speaking scores, the path diagram presented that perceived communication competence and personality indeed play roles in BE students' spoken English scores through WTC.

Furthermore, merely 5 percent of WTC related with spoken English performances. The number may seem to be too trivial to hardly make a huge change to BE students' spoken English learning in English classrooms. Nonetheless, bearing in mind MacIntyre et al. 's (1998) perspective that higher WTC can produce better English scores, the small number cannot be ignored as it is an indication contributing to the improvement of BE students' academic performances in spoken English. It may be presumed that different teacher practices are more influential than students' diverse WTC in making students communicate more in class. Taking T2 for the BEE sophomores as an example, the teacher had the highest f^2 of 0. 25 among the six instructors and thus it can be assumed that T2 actually makes their students speak more than the other teachers in English classrooms. In this case, it seems to be essential to observe the actual classroom teacher practices in later studies.

Fourthly, in MGSEM section, an analysis of the effect on oral English scores suggest that the BBE sophomores and juniors have somewhat different responses to the BEE students. Considering learning experience can affect BE students' WTC, T-tests uncovered that the BEE sophomores and juniors' WTC, extrovert personality and perceived communication competence levels were lower than the BEE freshmen. Also, the BEE sophomores and juniors' WTC, DC, affiliation and positive expectation of evaluation levels were lower than the freshmen. No obvious difference was shown in other variables for BE students.

The BBE sophomores and juniors, especially the BEE sophomores, had outstanding negative standard regression weights in the affiliation factor. It showed that they were not attached to their groups in the English language classrooms. It may be assumed that they dislike working in groups. Shifting to the teacher aspect, one reason attributed to the students' lack of affiliation may be the weak classroom context that the teacher provided to the students. In this sense, it can be speculated that the teacher in an English classroom might not give students enough time for group interactions or even dislikes them carrying out group work. It is possible that some teachers prefer the traditional way of lecturing instead of group communications. Further research can study this phenomenon through classroom observations and interviews with teachers and students, as the T-test results suggested the freshmen and the BEE and BBE sophomores and juniors differed in some WTC variables due to learning experience.

Nevertheless, model comparison across different instructors, programmes and years was invariant. But the model for instructors fitted somewhat less well than for programmes and years. The reason may be that the sample size for each of the six instructors are smaller than in two programmes and three years. In future, a longitudinal WTC study with each instructor for three years can be set up in order to enlarge the sample size of instructors and thus eliminate the small sample size effect. for instance, a study based on merging data collected from each instructor for three years.

6.3.2 Research Question Four—pedagogical changes

Based on answers obtained from Research Questions One and Three, Research Question Four "What pedagogical changes can be drawn to enhance BE students' WTC in English classrooms?" can be investigated. It was found that WTC only explained five percent of students' speaking scores. However, higher WTC can produce better English scores (MacIntyre et al. , 1998). Since teacher effects can be influential to students' speaking scores, it thus seems important for teachers in China to carry out effective strategies to arouse BE students' WTC and enhance their speaking scores. The majority of English classroom teachers are local Chinese teachers and non-native speakers of English are becoming more and more important in teaching English to speakers of other languages(TESOL). Along with the globalization of English (Bautista, 1997; Crystal, 1997; Kachru, 1992; Kirkpatrick, 2007; Liu, 1999), local Chinese teachers need to perform culturally-appropriate pedagogical changes to Chinese students. This implies that teachers in China can consider the teaching of China English while drawing on these pedagogical implications for enhancing BE students' WTC in spoken English in English lessons.

The seven variables of WTC, DC, anxiety, positive expectation of evaluation, affiliation, personality and perceived communication competence in the Chinese WTC model intertwined to influence BE students' WTC. BE students have low level of anxiety, but they have room to improve in the other six WTC variables. The low level of anxiety found is consistent with Garrott's (1995) and Shi's (2006) findings. They challenged the stereotyped view of the collectivistic outlook of the Chinese and considered the new generation is influenced by rapid social changes in China under the influence of globalization. Pedagogical changes were then proposed in DC, positive expectation of evaluation, affiliation, personality and perceived communication competence for enhancing WTC.

To begin with, since DC and affiliation were highly correlated, it is possible that the increase of affiliation and DC can lead to the enhancement of one another. Teachers can provide more opportunities for students to communicate (Rutherford & Ahlgren, 1990), especially in pair and group interactions. As affiliation had the highest extent/mean scores among the seven WTC variables, pair and group work suit students' need of affiliating to a particular group in the classroom. Next, in order to increase DC, teachers can provide challenges but attainable tasks and use authentic, real-world activities (Rutherford & Ahlgren, 1990), at the same time to motivate students' interest in speaking. For example, the teacher can ask students to make a speech after reading or sharing several stories related with what they are studying in the textbooks.

Then, it is essential to give proper feedback to students (Rutherford & Ahlgren, 1990) in order to improve self-perceptions about their own communication competence. Perceived communication competence and personality are indirectly linked with speaking scores through WTC. In this case, improved perceived communication competence may make students more extrovert and more willing to communicate (see Section 3.4.1.5). In addition, while students seek positive expectation of evaluation from others, teachers can help students by accommodating students in socially supportive environments (Paulsen, Bru &. Murberg, 2006), for instance, by forming less threatening small groups rather than the whole class (Kraft, 1985). Considering the four categories of BE students, more efforts can be made by English teachers in China to enhance their WTC. These points will be described in detail in the final chapter (see Section 9.2.4).

Also, learning experience can to some extent affect BE students' WTC. The BE sophomores and juniors' WTC decreased when compared with the BE freshmen. WTC lowered along with the decreasing of extrovert personality and perceived communication competence levels for BEE students, whereas DC, affiliation and positive expectation of evaluation for BBE students. Therefore, for the BE sophomores' and juniors' teachers, more attention should be paid to the decreasing variables of the two different BE programmes by emphasizing the strategies mentioned above.

6.4 Conclusion

This chapter includes the analysis of data obtained from Study One and Pilot Study Two. Data were first screened with missing data replaced by EM estimation and outliers excluded. Then confirmatory factor analysis and structural equation modeling as well as multi-group CFA and SEM are applied.

Also, descriptions of CFA and SEM data, such as mean scores and standard deviations were delineated. Later on, some issues regarding the findings of the seven-factor Chinese model, the cause of low anxiety, the relationship found between WTC and English speaking scores, and speculations about why the BBE sophomores and juniors had very different responses to the BEE students to some WTC factors, have been highlighted in the discussion section.

Finally, the research questions are answered regarding Chinese BE students' WTC at the personal level. The seven factors in the WTC model are inter-correlated with each other to influence BE students' WTC. Only low anxiety can enable BE students' WTC in spoken English learning. They have to conquer problems resulting from the other six factors in the WTC model in future. Though WTC as one of the seven factors in the model explained only five percent of students' spoken English scores, the findings cannot be neglected and broad pedagogical implications for enhancing Chinese BE students' WTC in spoken English in English classrooms (detailed in Chapter 9) are suggested for the identified four BE student categories according to high and low WTC as well as weak and supportive classroom context dichotomies. The next two chapters will examine both contextual and personal factors that affect BE students' WTC in English language lessons in detail on the basis of qualitative study findings, for the purpose of enriching the outcomes already found in this chapter from different dimensions.

Chapter 7
Study Two

This chapter will focus on analyzing the qualitative data obtained from documents, classroom observations and semi-structured interviews with teachers. Supportive and weak contexts were determined by horizontal codes of high and low WTC BE students and the vertical codes of Chinese WTC factors of group cohesiveness, teacher support, risk-taking, tolerance of ambiguity, affiliation, task-orientation, inhibited monitor and positive expectation of evaluation. Information about teacher and student participants will first be presented. Later on, findings and discussion are described. The outcomes will answer Research Questions Two, Three and Four related to contextual factors that assist and hinder BE students' WTC.

7. 1 *Participant information in qualitative studies*

The participants in Qualitative Studies Two and Three are described in Tables 14 and 15. Pseudonyms were used to refer to the twelve student and six teacher participants. In addition, the two interviewed teachers are marked with asterisks, indicating they were interviewees. One high WTC and one low WTC students from each grade of the BEE and BBE programmes in the years one to three were selected by their teachers. Due to the fact that the majority of BE students were female and also some male students declined to be involved in the study at the negotiation stage, it turned out that female students were twice as numerous as male students. Teacher participants were those, as pointed out by their students, who were teaching the Comprehensive English course, that is, six teachers from Grades One to Three of the two BE programmes. Meanwhile, it happened that there was an equal number of male and female teachers.

Table 14

Student participants in the Chinese WTC study

Number	Student name	Programme (year)	Sex	WTC	Classroom context
S1	Lan	BEE (1)	female	low	supportive
S2	Lai	BEE (1)	male	high	supportive
S3	Ni	BEE (2)	female	high	weak
S4	Huang	BEE (2)	female	low	weak
S5	Ling	BEE (3)	female	low	supportive
S6	Jing	BEE (3)	female	high	supportive
S7	Bing	BBE (1)	female	low	weak
S8	Bin	BBE (1)	male	high	weak
S9	Lu	BBE (2)	female	high	weak
S10	Zhou	BBE (2)	male	low	weak
S11	Xiao	BBE (3)	female	high	weak
S12	Yu	BBE (3)	male	low	weak

Table 15

Teacher participants in the Chinese WTC study

Number	Teacher name	Programme (year)	Sex	Classroom context	Interviewed
T1	Xue	BEE (1)	female	supportive	
T2	Yun	BEE (2)	female	weak	
T3	Moon	BEE (3)	male	supportive	*
T4	Ting	BBE (1)	female	weak	
T5	Lin	BBE (2)	female	weak	*
T6	Joe	BBE (3)	male	weak	

Note: * = being interviewed

Furthermore, the assessed supportive classroom contexts were in the year one and year three BEE programme. Other observed classroom contexts were rated as weak. Assessments of classroom contexts were based on observation results. Supportive or weak classroom context was defined and distinguished according to the two raters' assessments on whether tasks in a lesson (referring to type of an interaction and task difficulty) enabled or hindered BE students' WTC. Curriculum-related document analysis outcomes formed the basis .to assess task difficulty in classroom observations. Stimulated recalls outcomes complemented the observation results.

7.2 Document analysis outcomes

Curriculum materials were collected online, from the Teaching Affairs Office and the six teacher participants (see

Section 4. 6). The document analysis process includes "finding, selecting, appraising (making sense of), and synthesizing data" (Bowen, 2009). Firstly, these materials were timetables, educational scheme, and speaking skill assessment criteria from the university's website through intranet. Also, the official document that guided the design of these materials and the nation's teaching syllabus for BE students, was analyzed (see Section 4. 5). Secondly, the Teaching Affairs Office provided students' spoken English scores through personal emails. Thirdly, access to textbooks and student assignments was gained through teachers.

Though it was stated by the university's Teaching Affairs Office that BEE and BBE students indeed had some minor differences in teaching objectives, the two types of BE students had the same spoken English curriculum synthesized in Table 14. The curriculum was found to be a "means and ends" model (White, 1988) as mentioned in Section 4. 4. 2. Teaching aims, objectives, learning experiences and evaluation were the four aspects in this document analysis. The aims of spoken English instruction was not clear cut for BEE and BBE students, but more towards BEE students' aim of teaching spoken English in future for both BEE and BBE students. Also, it is obvious that only the BE freshmen and sophomores had the required spoken English objectives and learning experiences. Learning experiences are too general for teachers to follow rigidly to achieve the pre-specified objectives. As to evaluation, pronunciation and intonation test had the same weight as the conversation test.

Table 16

Synthesized spoken English curriculum

Aims	Requires BE students to be able to speak standard or relatively standard English in teaching, conversations, translations and speeches. At the same time, to master and use teacher language with basic teaching skills and methods to teach spoken English.
Objectives	Year one: to master good and basic skills in speaking, including pronunciation, intonation, syllable, stress, rhythm, tone and rhyming.
	Year two: to reach the requirements of Test for English Majors—Band 4(TEM 4), such as retell a story on the spot, make a keynote speech and a smooth conversation, and also be able to debate in English.
	Years three & four: none
Learning experiences	Year one: 1) emphasizes pronunciation, intonation and perception trainings. Students should consciously imitate and correct pronunciations, correctly grasp words' and sentences' common stress patterns, speak naturally with rhythm and intonation; 2) be able to ask questions, retell and carry out simple discussions around the content of a textbook; 3) be able to communicate on basic topics of daily life; 4) be able to express ideas correctly with no significant grammatical errors and with basic manners.
	Year two: 1) stresses the development of communication language and skills. Students can talk about daily life and social problems with native English speakers; 2) competent to express their ideas systematically, in depth and coherently; 3) with natural pronunciation and intonation, no significant grammatical errors, use words properly and expressed with good manners.
	Years three & four: none
Evaluation	Pronunciation and intonation test (50%) + conversation test (50%)

7.3　Classroom observation findings

In total six classes were observed and one each in each of the six teachers' classes. Two raters, Jane (a lecturer from an English department in another university) and I coded twenty-four classroom observation sheets. Types of interactive classroom tasks, task difficulty, as well as the twelve participant students' estimated WTC were coded (see Section 4.4.2). The criterion to rate the three elements on classroom observation sheets (see Appendix B) was based on raters' understanding of how the collected documents of course materials matched with students' cognitive and affective competencies in English learning. A trial video-recorded class was observed and rated before the actual observation as a training session on how to code. Turn-taking is an essential part of the communicative classroom discourse (Rymes, 2009). Thus, classroom observation sheets calculated the task time by taking turn-takings among different interlocutors into account.

The inter-rater agreement was computed first through bivariate correlation as the data were found to be normally distributed. The Pearson correlation was $r = 0.85$. Considering that two raters' scores can be highly correlated even when little agreement exists, one solution is to use intraclass correlation coefficient (Wuensch, 2010). Then, it was found that Cronbach's alpha was 0.92 and single measure intraclass correlation coefficient was 0.85 at the 95% confidence interval. In this case, all the above statistics were acceptable and greater than 0.7, indicating the existence of inter-rater reliability between the two raters' scores.

Findings of the summary of observed classroom interaction types, ranges of task difficulty as well as the high and low WTC students' percentages of WTC in the English classrooms are presented in Figures 17, 18 and 19.

Table 17

Correlations among interaction types, task difficulty and WTC

	1	2	3
Type of an Interaction	—		
Task Difficulty	0. 29 ** (0. 41 **)	—	
WTC (high/ low)	— /0. 24 * (0. 20 * /—)	−0. 41 ** / — (−0. 48 ** /—)	— /—

Note: statistics without parentheses were from rater one while within parentheses were from rater two; * * = correlation is significant at the 0.01 level (2—tailed); * = correlation is significant at the 0.05 level (2—tailed).

Table 17 shows the relationships among interaction types, task difficulty and high and low BE students' WTC. The Pearson correlation results of the two raters' scorings were similar in addressing the positive correlation between interaction types and task difficulty, revealing the negative correlation between high WTC students' WTC and task difficulty as well as no connection between low WTC students' WTC and task difficulty. According to Rater One's scorings, low WTC students' WTC positively associated with interaction types. However, different from Rater One's findings, high WTC students' WTC turned out to be negatively correlated with not only task difficulty, but also interaction types. Besides, low WTC students' WTC had no relation with both interaction types and task difficulty. In this case, it was agreed that the more towards the student-centered approach (such as I-C, I-G, I-I interactions in Figure 17) the pedagogy was, the harder the task was; and task difficulty had no influence on low WTC students, whereas high WTC students would like to conduct easy tasks instead of hard ones. Also, it was possible that both high and low WTC students' WTC might be more influenced by student-centered interactions rather than teacher-centered approaches.

Figure 18 shows that six types of classroom interactions were studied in the teacher-student and student-student cohorts and the two raters were consistent with the result. T-C, T-G and T-I are the three types of teacher interactions with the whole class, group and individual students, while I-C, I-G, I-I are the three types of student interactions with the whole class, group and individual students. Examples of the six types of interaction are teacher lecturing for the whole class in T-C, speaking with a group of students in T-G, individual student questioning in T-I, as well as student presentation in I-C, group work in I-G and pair work in I-I. As Figure 18 shows, two interactions of the teacher to the whole class as well as the teacher to individual student by the six teachers appeared as the commonly used types for them all, especially for Joe, Yun and Ting. This indicates that the classroom discourse was mainly controlled by these three English teachers.

According to Figure 18, it can be concluded that Moon's and Xue's classes were more "supportive" than other teachers' in the sense that not only teacher-student activities, but also more attention being paid to student-student interaction of student presentation, pair or group work. The three teachers, Jin, Moon and Xue, were similar in also using individual to individual

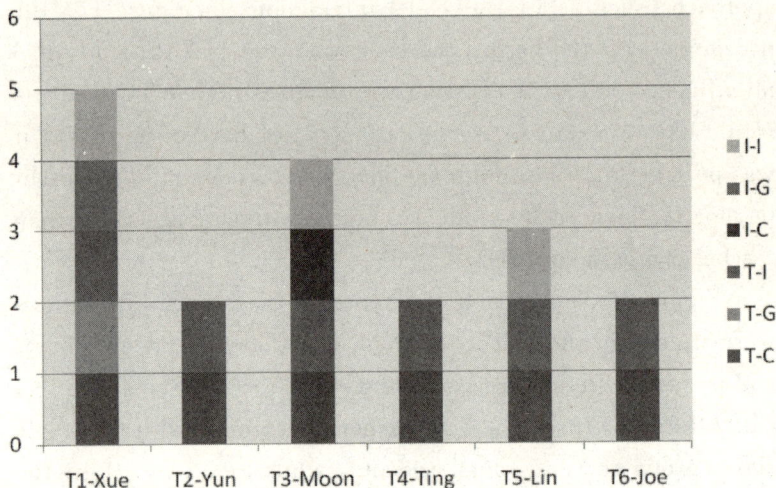

Figure 18. A summary of observed classroom interaction types.

Note：

  T-C＝the interaction between the teacher and the whole class；

  T-G＝the interaction between the teacher and a group of students；

  T-I＝the interaction between the teacher and an individual student；

  I-C＝the interaction between an individual student and the whole class；

  I-G＝the interaction between an individual student and a group of students；

  I-I＝the interaction between an individual student and another student.

student interactions besides teacher-student interactions，which means pair work here. Lin used pair work for only a short while during the class. Moreover，individual student to whole class interaction was used by Moon while Xue used teacher to group as well as individual to group interactions. In this case，the individual to the whole class interaction performed by Moon was student presentations and group works were actually carried out only in Xue's class.

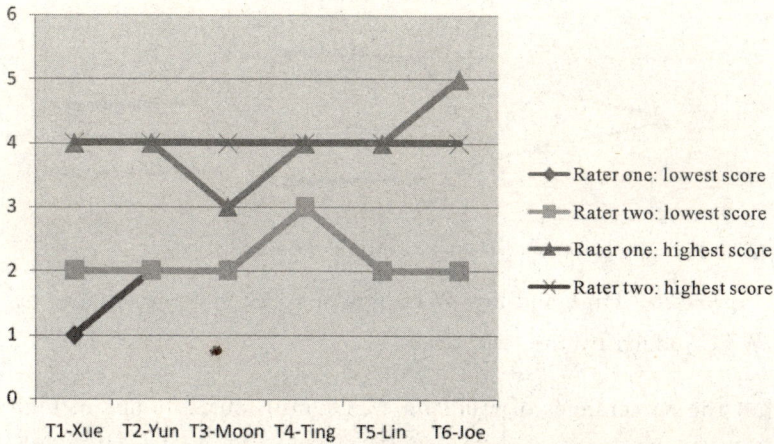

Figure 19. Ranges of classroom task difficulty rated by the two raters.

Figure 19 shows that the range of task difficulty was mostly between two to four with some fluctuations. This means that on the whole, task difficulty was mostly at the middle level and thus largely acceptable to students. While watching the video-recorded classes, it was clear that a class usually started with easy tasks and then more difficult tasks were introduced; however, the two raters had some minor disagreements while defining the task difficulty level of three instructors, Joe, Moon and Xue. The highest score differences for Joe was four by Rater Two and five by Rater One while for Moon it was three by Rater One and four by Rater Two. The lowest score difference for Xue was one by Rater One and two by Rater Two.

The two raters also judged high and low WTC students' extent of WTC towards each classroom interaction based on the assessment of the curriculum in document analysis. High and low WTC students were identified by their teachers. Figure 20

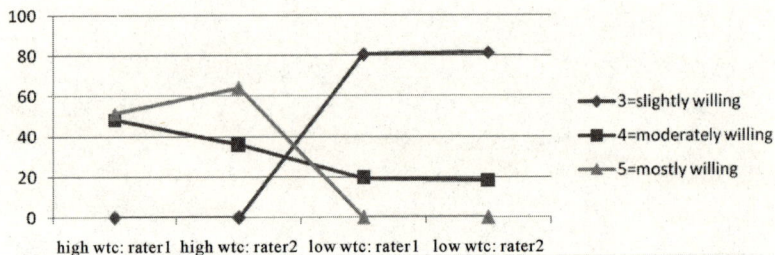

Figure 20. High and low WTC students' overall percentages of WTC judged by the two raters.

put the percentages of students' WTC into four columns of high WTC by Rater One, high WTC by Rater Two, low WTC by Rater One and low WTC by Rater Two. It is agreed by the two raters that high WTC students had WTC scores from moderately willing to mostly willing, whereas low WTC students had scores from slightly willing to moderately willing.

To summarize, the two raters were consistent in coding interaction types and WTC as shown by Figures 18 and 20; however, minor differences were found in their codes with regard to task difficulty in Figure 19. Ratings were distinct as to Xue's lowest score, Moon's highest score and Joe's highest score. Sample video extracts concerning the different ratings of task difficulty were then discussed and two observation excerpts were transcribed. At first, as to Xue's classroom observation, the task difficulty of only one classroom interaction was coded as the lowest score of 1(=extremely easy) by me while it was scored 2 (=mostly easy) by Jane. Class observation Excerpt One shows the interaction type was between the teacher and the whole class (T-C). The task was to ask students questions as an introduction or lead-in of a new unit to check if students had previewed the lesson. Rather easy questions of "How long?" and "She is small?" were asked by Xue. The teacher actually did not seek the answers from students. Instead, she was trying to attract students' attentions into the new topic. I thought it was a completely easy task while Jane's view was that with the teacher's purposeful setting of the introduction, the task cannot be simply regarded as extremely easy.

[Classroom observation Excerpt One]

T1: There is a storyteller. Maybe you would like doing it, um I mean, how long? She's lot younger, she's eighteen, I mean ...

C: (Laugh)

T1: She is small?

C: Yeah.

T1: Well, people can really tell she's silent ...

Disagreement over video extracts in Moon's classroom observation sheets were one about a student's prepared speech to the whole class (I-C), and the other one about the dialogue between the teacher and a student (T-I). In the I-C interaction, the task was to examine how well a student prepared the homework: speech with power points at the beginning of a lesson. A student made a prepared speech on the topic of how to live your college life without making the required power points. He described his understanding about the college life that most students experienced while standing in front of the lecture desk, facing all his classmates and the teacher. The speech itself was not hard to make as it was about the speaker's personal experience as a college student. Also, no specialized or ambiguous words appeared in his language. Thus I rated the task as 3 (=slightly difficult).

However, Jane considered that the exposure to the whole class for such a longer time than usual during the five or more minutes' speech was an affective challenge for the student, for example, causing the anxious feeling which hindered the students' performance. Therefore, she rated the task as 4 (=moderately difficult).

In the T-I interaction, another task, which related with students' real lives, was carried out by Moon as a lead-in of a new unit to check if students had previewed the lesson. The individual student nominated by the teacher stood up to answer a main question and some follow-up questions. The questions were about college life, which was the topic of the new learning unit in the textbook. I rated the task as 3 (=slightly difficult) out of similar reasons to those mentioned above. Though no nervous expressions were shown in the student's face, Jane believed the student might be anxious when nominated by the teacher to carry out a task. Thus she rated the task as 4 (=moderately difficult).

[Classroom observation Excerpt Two]

T3: If you are not in college, what will you do? Let me ask some students please. (Then named a student)

I: Of course in studying.

T3: Why do you prefer to study?

I: I prefer study so I insist.

T3: Study while work?

I: If I didn't study, what should I do? ... I can't find a good job.

Moreover, distinct ratings of task difficulty occurred regarding two video extracts of the teacher Joe's classroom observation. The two extracts were common in the nature of the task, which consisted of translation works. The T-I interaction was made up of Joe nominating individual students to translate some sentences in the textbook. The two students, one in each extract, seemed to be reluctant to stand up to translate. Translation works, as the textbook suggested, required the mastery of relatively advanced bilingual (English and Chinese) knowledge, which were of high cognitive demand even for those BE students in senior years. Meanwhile, mediating the long pause a student had to act before coming out with the answer, the translation task was quite difficult. In this case, I rated tasks as 5 (= mostly difficult); nonetheless, Jane viewed translation works as a requirement of the course established by the curriculum and thus it must be within the reach of the students' competencies, therefore she rated the task as 4 (= moderately difficult).

In summary, classroom observations found the relations of interaction types, task difficulty and WTC. Except some differences while rating WTC and task difficulty, the two raters had good inter-rater agreement in coding the classroom observation sheets. The more towards the student-centered interaction types, the harder the tasks were; however, high WTC students tended to prefer easier tasks. High WTC had the WTC scores from moderately willing to mostly willing while low WTC had scores from slightly willing to moderately willing.

7.4　Teacher interview results

The two teacher interviews sought to find out different reasons underlying the construction of weak and supportive classroom

Table 18

Teacher interview comparison outcome

	Classroom context	Course teaching experience	Issue of classroom interaction types	Task difficulty	Common point
T5-Lin	Weak	New	Problem in using individual student nomination	Test preparation with complaints from students	No group works used
T3-Moon	Supportive	Many years	Successes in using a scaffolding way of questioning, prepared speech and two way discussions	Flexible use of textbooks and authentic materials with attainable tasks	

contexts for BE students' WTC in spoken English. In line with classroom observations, the two teacher interview transcripts were compared with regard to classroom interactions and task difficulty. Also, their teaching experiences were compared.

Table 18 shows the comparison outcome of Lin's and Moon's interview transcripts regarding the assessment of the classroom context, course teaching experience, issues of classroom interaction types, type difficulty and common point. Lin and Moon were interviewed after their English classes were observed. Lin, a female and the instructor of the BBE sophomores, was assessed as providing a "weak" classroom context, which means weak support for students' spoken tasks. Though she had many years' experience in teaching English at secondary and tertiary levels, this academic year was her first time teaching the Comprehensive English course. Different from Lin, Moon, a male, teaching the BEE juniors, with an assessed supportive classroom context, was the dean of the Foreign

Languages Department and had many years' experience in teaching the Comprehensive English course. Table 18 shows that the analyzed interview data suggested Lin's challenges in using individual student nomination and receiving complaints from students in test preparation versus Moon's successes in using scaffolded questioning, prepared speech, two way discussions and the flexible use of textbooks and authentic materials with attainable tasks in English classroom instructions with regard to interaction types and task difficulty. Lin and Moon had the similar idea of purposeful neglecting group work to compensate for more exercises on the national English exams for BE students.

7.4.1 Teacher with weak classroom context

Lin mentioned that she was very excited and ambitious at the beginning of teaching this fundamental and compulsory course for BBE students. She was previously trained in UK as a postgraduate student, and wished to fill her class with an innovative and active atmosphere by using her teaching philosophy.

"This class, for me, means I finally get the chance to teach the Comprehensive English course. I really wish students can be involved in communicative activities... My master thesis conducted in UK... was to cultivate students' lifelong learning abilities ... At present, my classroom design is more or less influenced by what I learned at that time. "

But as time went by, she found that her students were not as enthusiastic as her about actively participating in classroom activities. Students were quite unhappy when they were called upon to stand up to answer questions in her English classroom. Frustrated feelings surged out when a student badly assessed her efforts.

"The result is that some students in their end of semester assessment of teachers wrote that: What I hate most is that the teacher calls my name in the class; you should know I'm in the university now ... Since then, I cannot call their names freely."

Recently, she also made some efforts to improve her students' spoken English, but ended up with negative feedback from her students. Since the oral test of TEM 4 was approaching, Lin assigned more after-class homework to her students. Lin paid much attention to TEM 4, which is taken by BE students in the second year of their study and is a prerequisite for taking TEM 8. Unfortunately, her students were not cooperating with her work.

"Because the oral test is coming, before, when I said to assign tasks, they rather disliked it. He/she said I'm a university student. That means this is a university he/she needs to be more relaxed. Then I play a not very good role. It seems that I require too much of them ... "

As an experienced teacher in teaching secondary students, Lin reflected on the current teaching problems in comparison with her past secondary teaching experience.

"Some students are willing to communicate, but I feel that the majority of the students just don't like you act like that. You don't have the same right as a teacher in a secondary school to name whoever that you want. This is a practical issue, and I feel for me this is a challenge."

Eventually, she attributed the reason forming BBE students'

lower WTC than secondary school students to the distinct age characteristics. Inferring from her words, students in university are not as submissive to teachers as secondary students.

"I, initially think that (in) Comprehensive English course, you have to be very concentrated, should be with very high WTC, but in reality I think that what I did most successfully in secondary school cannot work out here; characteristics in age are different."

Meanwhile, Lin complained that another reason causing her students' low WTC in speaking English in class was that those BBE students had no pronunciation lessons before. Also, the spoken English class they received in their first year given by native English speaking teachers was of little help to their improvement in spoken English. In this case, it can be concluded that students' low spoken English proficiency was one cause of their low WTC in classrooms.

"The class hasn't attended any pronunciation class. The pronunciation bases are quite distinct, and (students) don't have specialized fix of their mistakes. At that time it was out of no reasons that the classes' time was not enough, and this (pronunciation class) was cut out ... Probably this class without pronunciation training was the first one in history after the establishment of the university ...

"Our children, when in their freshman year, had spoken English class with a native English speaking teacher. But the teacher, according to students', was of little help. So he/she thinks that his/her (spoken) English is just so so.

"As to group work, I'm willing to do ... But I don't present it much... but as I view that kind of talking between students feeling, I personally think, I feel that students' involvement is not the same with primary and secondary students'. He/she won't participate in (a group work activity) just for a little star or flower ... Normally and often, I feel that kind of activity, or to say easily speak out things are few now. "

After the observation of Lin's class, I found that the lesson was carried out by mostly individual student nomination and pair work. While referring to students' other interactive tasks in classrooms, Lin suggested that as the oral test of TEM 4 were coming in May, it was not possible to conduct, for instance, group work. "A little star or flower" here refers to rewards or encouragements from the teacher. Students in Lin's class were reluctant to participate in group work even if with rewards or encouragements from the teacher.

7.4.2 *Teacher with supportive classroom context*

Moon considers current BE students were not as good as past students with such high WTC in the English classroom.

"Our students in the past have much better awareness of learning, autonomy of learning and way of learning than current students; this is without doubt. As a teacher, I deeply feel about this point. The reason is multi-facets ... "

Moon had his way of questioning students. An instance of this way of questioning can be found in classroom observation Excerpt Two. This technique was to assure that the task was attainable and within the reach of an individual student. In this case, Moon scaffolded his students' cognitive development in L2 learning without suffering their feelings in English classrooms.

"What kinds of questions are suitable for him/her, I will

name him/her. If the question is not fit for him/her (but I still ask), it will make one more tortured ... My first question is the basis, and if the student can answer then my second question will be asked, finally the third question is the real question ... but with some accommodations, (for) different targeted students, (I have to) choose which question to ask first. If the student is really good, then I will ask the third question first ... "

Meanwhile, Moon was distinct from other teachers in using what he called "prepared speech", which is actually a student presentation to the whole class. In his prepared speech, no notes were allowed to be taken to the front stage and the student was required to deliver the out of class prepared speech to the audience with confidence and fluent English, ideally with power points. After a student's speech, questions were asked by both the teacher and the other students. Also, the student audience can exchange their ideas with their partners to think up questions. In this case, there are presenter's interactions with both the teacher (T-I) and students (I-C and I-I).

"In prepared speech, there are interactions with students, between the professor and the students, two ways."

With regard to course materials, Moon was flexible in using textbooks as well as relevant extracurricular, authentic and real world materials. Authenticity is "(1) provenance and authorship of the text; (2) original communicative and socio-cultural purpose of the text; (3) original context (e. g. , its source, socio-cultural context) of the text; (4) learning activity engendered by the text; and (5) learners' perceptions of and attitudes to the text and the activity pertaining to it" (Mishan, 2005, p. 18). When asked how he managed the teaching, he said:

"... This schedule is a basic planning, an outline, but I absolutely not completely follow the teaching schedule. Because the classroom changes ... "

Then, he gave an example of his flexible use of the textbooks for the purpose of activating students' thoughts. Instead of rigidly following the syllabus, Moon's classes were dynamic and based on students' needs.

"According to the teaching syllabus, this unit should be finished using six classes. I can manage to finish in six classes. But not absolutely follow the teaching syllabus. Maybe in the first class I only teach a half of the planned lesson, but while I teach, I possibly integrate the third and the fourth class into the first class. That absolutely has dynamics, very big, but the overall time doesn't change ... Activation is very important, especially for English teaching in higher education ... "

In addition, since having observed the use of extracurricular, authentic materials in his class, the question of how often extracurricular materials were used popped up. Moon pointed out the relevance is definitely there between his frequent applications of authentic materials and the textbooks.

Despite the applications of many interactive and effective teaching methods, while I was curious about why not using group work in his class, Moon said it was not a necessary thing to do with seniors. Rather, he would like to put more efforts into pushing his students writing essays in order to gain higher scores in TEM 4. TEM 8 mentioned by Moon is the highest ranked examination for BE students in Chinese universities and is usually taken in the final year of their English studying.

"Seniors don't do it. I think no (need to do it)... It's a waste of too much time. That is to go back and write essays. I assign 8 essays in a semester. All are exposition, and also the words ought to be between 800 and 1,500 ... That's why my students perform well in TEM 8. "

7.5　Discussion

Findings of documents as well as classroom observations and semi-structured interviews with teachers show the contextual factors contributing to BE students' WTC, unfolding the map of how various classroom interaction types and task difficulty build BE students' different extents of WTC. It can also be inferred from the findings that the influential roles of course designers and classroom teachers in course design and implementation can greatly impinge on classroom interaction types and task difficulty. The improved classroom interaction types and task difficulty can then affect BE students' WTC. Discussions concerning the findings will be presented in the following sections to answer the three research questions.

7.5.1　Research Question Two—contextual factors that facilitate or hinder BE students' WTC

Study Two in fact mainly probed into the societal context factor, especially teacher support in Wen and Clément's (2003) Chinese conceptualization of WTC. Results show deficiencies in documents (see Section 7.2) and teachers' decision-making in interaction types and task difficulty (see Sections 7.3 & 7.4) can influence students' WTC. Also, teachers should take the similarities and differences between high and low WTC students in interaction types and task difficulty, as well as omission of group work into account while wishing to raise students' WTC in spoken English in English lessons. The second research question of what factors facilitate or hinder BE students' WTC can be answered through three facets. In order to narrow down the distance between high and low WTC BE students, more room needs to be filled with suitable spoken English curriculum as well as adjusted task interaction types and task difficulty within the reach of BE students for the purpose of enhancing BE students' WTC.

7.5.1.1 Deficiencies in documents

At the outset, the document analysis outcomes imply some deficiencies in the design of the spoken English curriculum. Both BEE and BBE students had the same spoken English requirements stated in the curriculum and assessment criteria; however, to design CLT curriculum for learners, the first and foremost thing is to identify learner needs (Zhang, 2006). Since BEE and BBE students have different future career orientations, it seems to be inappropriate to cultivate both BE programmes in the same way of English Education, without the mentioning of Business English.

Meanwhile, no specified requirements of curriculum focus and manifestation were designated for the BE juniors and seniors. The missing information means there is no basic instruction guidelines for the junior and senior teachers to follow in their English classrooms. It is possible that these teachers will be confused about what actually should be carried out in English classrooms, causing their diverse ways of spoken English teaching while making decisions of performing what types of interactions and what levels of task difficulty. Thus, as to spoken English course designers and implementers, more explicit and complete spoken English curriculum design needs to be developed.

7. 5. 1. 2 Teacher support in interaction types and task difficulty

Secondly, as the classroom observation results found the relationships among WTC, interaction types and task difficulty, this indicates that teachers' decision making in interaction types and task difficulty can influence their students' WTC. The teacher interview comparison also indicated the importance of carrying out suitable interaction types and task difficulty. To learn from Moon, supportive classroom context for developing spoken English build on the diverse T-S and S-S ways of effective interactions embedding the considerations of students' spoken English competencies as well as the flexible use of textbooks and authentic materials with attainable tasks.

There is a need to use both authentic materials and text-based materials. Though text-based materials are valued for being tailor-made to be easy-to-comprehend for developing students' language abilities (Bell, 2005), weaknesses of these constructed materials are obvious regarding the development of communicative competence in such as being less interesting and not bring the real world reading to students (Horwitz, 2008; Shrum & Glisan, 2000). Rather, interesting and real world authentic materials are found to be beneficial for increasing students' motivation in L2 learning (Guariento & Morley, 2001; Oguz & Bahar, 2008).

However, in this study, only two out of six teachers were judged as establishing supportive classroom environments for BE students. Representative extracts of weak classroom contexts in a large extent the T-S interactions between the teacher and the individual student, as well as those between the teacher and the whole class. In contrast, teachers with assessed supportive classroom contexts used various types of interactions frequently, not only between the teacher and students, but also among students.

7.5.1.3 *Similarities and differences between high and low WTC students*

Furthermore, high and low WTC students had some similarities and differences regarding interaction types and task difficulty. Students' WTC was assessed to be from slightly willing to mostly willing, but low WTC students had more percentages of slightly willing while high WTC students had more percentages of moderately willing and mostly willing. High and low WTC students were similar in more inclination to accept a student-centered approach, for instance, group work.

Unexpectedly, task difficulty had no influence on low WTC students, whereas high WTC students would like to conduct easy tasks instead of hard ones. It can be assumed that high WTC BE students' attachment to easier tasks out of their face-oriented approach and perfectionism inside English classrooms. Maladaptive perfectionism, expressed in such as over-concerns about mistakes and doubts about performances, was found to be positively correlated with burnout for Chinese undergraduates (Zhang, Gan & Cham, 2007). To avoid losing face and burnout, and also afraid of attaining negative evaluation from the teacher and classmates in the English classroom, it was possible that a high WTC BE student tended to choose a safe way, that is, to conduct those easy-to-accomplish tasks.

7.5.1.4 Omission of group work in English lessons

Thirdly, group work is the interaction type excluded by teachers in English lessons, as the two teacher interviews suggested. Lin's and Moon's reasons for leaving out group work were different in that Lin thought it was a temporary period for neglecting group work as it was not required in the oral test, while Moon mentioned it was completely a waste of time to employ group work in seniors' English classrooms, considering his deliberation of replacing group work with individual essay writing. Nevertheless, Lin's and Moon's perspectives were out of the same reason of making their English classroom instructions towards the examination-orientated approach in order to prepare their students for the two important national tests of TEM 4 and TEM 8.

Regardless of Lin's and Moon's dismissal of group work, it was evidenced in classroom observation coding result that both high and low WTC BE students preferred a student-centered approach to a teacher-centered approach. This finding is consistent with Hamm et al. 's (2011) in suggesting the importance of teacher supports to attune students' affiliation through the application of group work.

7.5.2 Research Question Three—interactions between personal and contextual factors

This study's findings regarding the contextual factors that facilitate or inhibit students' WTC in spoken English are in line with Cao's (2011) findings. Mediating Cao's three dimensions of contextual WTC, findings of Study Two mainly fit in the environmental (i. e. topic, task type, interlocutor, teacher and class interactional pattern) and linguistic aspects (i. e. language proficiency). But "reliance on L1" in the linguistic aspect in Cao's model seems not to be an influential factor, as BE students mostly speak English instead of Chinese in the lessons. It can be referred that the effective use of instructional strategies with suitable interaction types and attainable task difficulty environmentally and linguistically can increase BE students' WTC. Otherwise, inappropriate application of these strategies can inversely hinder BE students' WTC in English classrooms.

7.5.3 Research Question Four—pedagogical changes

To answer the last research question, pedagogical recommendations can be made in two aspects: curriculum development and the adjustment of task interaction types and task difficulty, to enhance BE students' WTC. In addition, techniques to obtain students' compliance in tasks are considered.

7.5.3.1 Curriculum development

To begin with, it is vital to clarify the curriculum for students in different BE programmes in order to guide their studies in different disciplines, since instrumental motivation plays a crucial role for Chinese students (Warden & Lin, 2000; Liu, 2007). Nonetheless, for a practical teacher, it is not what motivation should be focused on, rather how motivation can be increased (Dörnyei, 2001).

While considering students' greater application of

instrumental motivation as well as the idea of BEE and BBE students having different future career orientations, apart from designing spoken English curriculum for BEE students, an integrated approach to teach business English propounded by Zhang (2007) can be adopted. Zhang proposed a curriculum design composed of the two perspectives of English for Specific Purposes (ESP) and business discourse studies. Two current perspectives in the teaching of Business English are in fashion, since there is a tendency towards content-based or even research-based teaching practices. The purpose of the curriculum is to educate business expertise rather than just learning English language knowledge and skills.

7.5.3.2 Adjustment of task interaction types and difficulty

Then, to bring about culturally-appropriate classroom communication to provoke Chinese BE students' WTC, the mixed use of communicative and non-communicative activities, involving the neglected application of group work will be discussed with regard to task interaction types (Richards, 2006). Also, the use of attainable but challenging tasks and authentic materials will be helpful for improving the quality of task difficulty. Richards (2006) considered CLT today in the world is changed with the integrated use of classical CLT practices and traditional instructional approaches, implying the possible combined use of communicative and non-communicative interactions to reach the aim of effective learning. Thus, teachers' discarding of group works may be cautioned.

Moreover, for facilitating BE students' WTC in spoken English, English classroom teachers can perform attainable speaking tasks harmonizing with the Chinese culture. For reducing students' anxiety in tasks in English lessons, studies by Timina and Butler (2011) and Liu and Jackson (2008) suggest the same perspective with this study: making proper and interesting task topics.

However, tasks should not be merely reachable, but also must be challenging for enabling BE students' WTC in spoken English. Classroom observation result showed that high WTC students tended to conduct easy tasks out of the face-saving purpose. Nevertheless, it seems to be essential to perform a series of tasks or called a task chain from the easy ones to difficult ones for students' cognitive development (Wang, 2010). Thus, high WTC students' tendency to deal with only easy tasks definitely can exert a side-effect on students' speaking skill development.

In addition, authentic tasks can be helpful for facilitating students' spoken English and enable their WTC in speaking. This point was evidenced in Moon's interview transcript about the construction of supportive classroom context. Especially for communicative tasks, tasks should be authentic for communicative purpose (Wang, 2010). Nevertheless, it is almost impossible to fully reduplicate authentic real world activities. Nunan (2001) points out that while putting English used in everyday life into the classroom, the authentic level is actually decreased to some extent. In this case, Wang suggests that classroom teachers can try to deliver authentic tasks at the utmost level.

7.5.3.3　*Techniques to obtain students' compliance*

In addition, considering students' unwillingness to cooperate with the teacher in Lin's situation, eleven prosocial behavior alteration techniques (BATs) can be drawn to obtain students' compliance (Paulsel, 2004). The eleven prosocial BATs are about potential rewarding strategies, of "immediate reward from behavior, deferred reward, reward from others, self-esteem, responsibility to class, normative rules, altruism, peer modeling, teacher modeling, expert teacher, and teacher feedback" (p. 45). However, Kearney et al. (1984) pointed out that the effective use of these strategies depends on the judgment of specific contexts as well as teaching experiences and teachers' reflections on the applied strategies. The next chapter will show the findings of Study Three to fill Cao's (2011) individual dimension of the contextual WTC.

Chapter 8
Study Three

This chapter will focus on analyzing the qualitative data obtained from student narratives, stimulated recalls and semi-structured interviews with students. The vertical Chinese WTC codes of group cohesiveness, teacher support, risk-taking, tolerance of ambiguity, affiliation, task-orientation, inhibited monitor, and positive expectation of evaluation and the horizontal codes of high and low WTC were used to probe into the formation of the four categories of BE students at the personal level. The outcomes will answer Research Questions One, Three and Four related to personal factors that assist or hinder BE students' WTC. Then, discussion will be unfolded. Furthermore, Studies One and Two results will be integrated in this chapter to try to solve the research problem.

8.1 *Student narratives*

The twelve student participants were asked after classroom observations to hand in their narratives of their past and present spoken English learning experiences concerning their WTC in English classrooms when they came in for interviews. In total, eleven student narratives were collected. Yu, a BEE junior with low WTC, refused to write since he mentioned that he was quite busy with some extracurricular activities. Other students' information can be found in Table 14 in Section 7. 1. Collected students' writings were grouped into four varieties according to the four categories of students divided by WTC and classroom contextual factors. Students' narratives in the four varieties were re-storied by using the researcher's voice and some comments on the rewrite stories are attached at the end of each subsection. Table 19 summarizes the main points of the comments with emphasis on the students' present English classroom learning experience. A sample narrative from Zhou with low WTC and weak classroom context can be referred to in Appendix G.

Table 19

Student narratives of past and present English classroom experiences

WTC student factor	Classroom context factors	
	Weak, not supportive	Strong, supportive
High WTC	1. Past: weak or supportive contexts.	2. Past: teacher-centered approach.
	Present: all unsatisfied with current classroom context; somewhat boring; teacher-dominated lecturing; had to use self-study after the class.	Present: all praised the student-centered approach.

Continued

WTC student factor	Classroom context factors	
	Weak, not supportive	Strong, supportive
	3. Past: weak or supportive contexts.	4. Past: weak or supportive contexts.
Low WTC	Present: all owned desire to communicate; gloomy if can't answer a question; limited class time to assimilate specialized knowledge through just listening to the teacher; deprived chances of speaking by the other students; needed more waiting time before speaking out.	Present: praised fair provision of spoken chances; complained headaches caused by unaccustomed interaction types at the beginning of the study; hindrances in introvert personality and excessive positive expectation of evaluation.

8.1.1 *High WTC and weak context*

The BEE sophomore Ni and three BBE students, the freshman Bin, the sophomore Lu and the junior Xiao, had high WTC though in weak classroom contexts. Ni compared the past and present teachers' different ways of instruction to start an English class, suggesting the current classroom context for learning spoken English is not as good as that in the past. In high school, the beginning of a class was the warming up section. The teacher would recall last class's language points through interaction with students, mainly through a dialogue between the teacher and students. When teaching vocabulary, the teacher asked students to repeat after the tape. However, often, the comprehensive English course now has no warming up or review section. It is what the students should "self-study" after the class.

Bin's writing didn't mention anything about his past spoken English learning experience, but he stated that he was lazier than before. His high WTC is out of his motivation to speak English and in fact he likes speaking English. Thus, he always joins in some English speaking contests. But he noted that he didn't want to do exercises in English classrooms and he would "self-study" to improve his spoken English.

Lu wrote that the current spoken English learning was full of dreadful exercises for passing TEM 4, whereas the past English classroom stimulated her active participation in reading and answering questions. In high school, when an English class started, the teacher would first ask students to follow her in reading aloud new words. Because of her enthusiasm towards the English language, she would loudly, clearly and actively read the new words out. Then, the teacher led them to the understanding of the content. Firstly, she would ask them to read through the whole text and then ask questions. Then, she would ask several questions according to the main idea of the content. The teacher would name students' names one by one. Sometimes, a row of students answered the same question. Lu thought that reading was a very interesting thing, and answering questions can stimulate the active atmosphere of the whole class and better improve the classroom learning efficiency. As to the current English classroom, since it is the second semester of the second year, students have to face TEM 4 and the oral test of TEM 4. Each class's task is to do exercises and then analyze exercises. Lu complained it is "somewhat boring".

Xiao's past and present spoken English learning experiences are quite similar and mostly covered with teacher lecturing with few chances for practicing spoken English. In the past, from the start till the end of the class, almost all was teacher lecturing. Occasionally, there were "little episodes", which means interactions between the teacher and the students. However, she mentioned that the disadvantages of such classrooms were obvious, as student centeredness and creativity were hardly expounded. For Xiao, at that time, maybe her interest in English learning, her classroom communications with the teacher were relatively numerous. After entering the university, English courses are diversified. Some classes still follow the same teaching mode as in high school. Xiao used veiled words of "some classes... " to refer to the comprehensive English she is having now.

Despite the weak or supportive classroom context the students had in the past, the four high WTC BE students all described their lack of satisfaction about the present English classroom context. Ni and Bin sought to "self-study" after the class for help in order to enhance their spoken English. Lu directly pointed out the current classroom is "somewhat boring". Xiao discreetly suggested the present English classroom as one of "some classes" that still follow the teacher lecturing instructional style.

8.1.2 High WTC and supportive context

There were two high WTC BEE students, the freshman Lai and the junior Jing, in the supportive classroom contexts. Lai's past English learning experience was teacher-centered with few opportunities to speak English; however, the present English learning is more student-centered with more chances to speak

English. In high school, his English study was passive. Basically his role was to follow the teacher's instructions. He listened to what the teacher told him to listen to; he learnt what the teacher told him to learn. At present, the college study is active. Sometimes, the teacher's classroom teaching can even be student-centered. Even if the teacher does not say a word in a class, students can speak out their minds freely, pushing the classroom learning to a climax: with active student participation in tasks.

In line with Lai, Jing reported similar experiences to Lai. Jing's past English classroom learning was mostly following the audio-lingual mode, emphasizing the study of vocabulary and grammar. The current classroom environment differed from the past classroom environment in that more communicative forms and equipment supported the realization of communicative language teaching. Jing evaluated the present experience of English learning positively. She remembered that the English classroom at that time didn't involve lots of fantastic classroom activities, games or multi-media tools to continuously strengthen and stimulate students' learning activeness. Most teachers often used the relatively traditional ways to teach vocabulary and grammar and the courses. Now, college teaching forms are various and play a positive role in cultivating students' thinking, communicative and cognitive abilities. The flexibility of the classroom forms such as presentation, debate, pair work and group work all can provide good ways for students to explore their inner potentiality and continuously enhance English learning quality by themselves.

The two high WTC students are quite similar in their past

and present English classroom learning in spoken English. The move from the previous teacher-centered classroom context to the current student-centered context supports their spoken English learning. Both of them highly praised the present classroom context at the end of their narratives.

8.1.3 *Low WTC and weak context*

The BEE sophomore Huang and two BBE students, the freshman Bing and the sophomore Zhou, had low WTC in the weak classroom contexts. Huang suggested that spoken English was hardly used in both past and present classrooms. Her high school comprised exam preparation and all instructions were for meeting the needs of passing the national examination to university. The teacher used his own ways to combine all the teaching content. Students' thoughts just followed the teacher and there was no need to think too much, as the study was considered to remember knowledge. Currently, though the study mode shifted from the past teacher-dominated model with the aim of passing exams for entering into universities to the present teacher-guided self-study model, English classrooms were occupied with direct knowledge delivery listened by teachers. She considered that in university, self-study is very important. Teachers' instructions just cover the general matters. Classroom time for learning is not enough. The college courses tend to be more specialized and be hard to understand, and cannot be mastered just through simply listening to it.

Though at present Bing still desired to communicate in classrooms, her chances of speaking English were reduced by some other excellent students in her class and caused her low

WTC. She did not have such low WTC in English classrooms before. In the past, the English teacher helped her a lot and at that time she was very active with high WTC in English lessons. In the past, at first, she hated English because she perceived her spoken English proficiency was low compared with the other classmates, as she didn't receive after-class English training. In classes, she was not very active to answer questions. But her English teacher was there to help her. Gradually, she started to be more hard-working. Then her English score went up tremendously. Also, she became more confident and active in lessons. At present, she still found that in the university there are many excellent students. They are very active and their English scores are also high. They always have already answered questions before she is about to do.

Zhou mentioned his decreased enthusiasm of learning spoken English in the current classroom context compared with the past. While learning English in middle and high schools, actually he was always extremely enthusiastic. He noted that it was because he himself was very interested in English. Three types of students' ways of question answering were expressed. Teacher nomination was the worst type as it sometimes triggered his "gloomy" feeling. The other two types of spontaneous answering and a special way of answering in horizontal and vertical lines were favored by him. After entering the university, he feels his enthusiasm in learning English fell remarkably. He guessed it was because the way of learning changed or the teacher's instructions were not suitable for him. Zhou's narrative can be seen in Appendix G.

The three identified low WTC students experienced weak or

supportive classroom contexts before, but now are in weak classroom contexts. Even as low WTC students, they had a desire to communicate and the weak classroom context can reduce their willingness to communicate in English lessons. For instance, in the past, Zhou expressed the "gloomy" feeling if he couldn't answer a question. Huang found it was hard to understand the "more specialized" knowledge by just listening to the teacher during the limited English class time. To some extent, this point explains that the present instructions cannot match with her English proficiency. Moreover, Bing's apparent comparison of the past supportive classroom context and the present weak classroom context suggests the teacher should give students more chances and more waiting time in classroom interactions.

8.1.4 *Low WTC and supportive context*

The two low WTC BEE students, the freshman Lan and the junior Ling, were in the supportive classroom contexts. The teachers Lan encountered in the past and present English classroom learning settings were supportive. Taking the teacher in the second semester of high school for example, Lan found her powerpoint presentations were very fascinating and also the lessons often involved some classroom games or team contests. Thus, they always stimulated students' mood. In the university, the teacher leads students step by step towards the development of more speaking and practices, making the efforts to give them chances to let them experience various ways of interactions in English lessons. Almost each class has diverse forms of presentations—news broadcasting, text analysis, text review, role plays, outdoor news investigation and videotaping, movie review and so on. At the beginning, these things make her feel "headaches" and gave her no idea of what to do. Almost all things have to be found out by her. She thought that the teacher is responsible and teaches well. But this is university. She cannot always let the teacher focus on her and remind her while standing next to her. Later on, she became familiar with this kind of lesson.

Ling wrote that the most influential factor that impacted on the extent of her WTC in the past and present was how "fair" the teacher was to her in English lessons. The more attention and chances the teacher gave her, the more active she would be. Furthermore, she attributed her low WTC to her "cowardly" "super unconfident" personality in English language learning. As to open-ended questions, she was rarely willing to answer. Meanwhile, her repeated worries of making "mistakes" reflected her unwillingness to take risks while her fear of being "laughed at" by her classmates showed that she expected positive evaluations from her classmates. Considering her past learning experiences, unlike the others who refer to these in secondary schools, she mentioned only the first year of university. At that time, she was relatively active. But then she found that the teacher belonged to the biased type, especially taking care of the boys in the class at ordinary times in team contests. The teacher always ignored the team Ling was in. Then, as time passed, she became more and more uninterested in learning or speaking out in English classrooms. She prefers the current English teacher as he is relatively fair. Thus, when she thinks she knows the answer, she will offer to respond. She doesn't dare to use

English to communicate with classmates or talk in a group because she is afraid that she will make grammatical errors or other mistakes.

The two low WTC students in the supportive classroom context experienced diverse classroom situations in the past. Supportive classroom contexts in the past and present are welcomed by Lan, which certainly plays an optimistic role in her spoken English in English lessons. However, in the present study in university, insufficient teacher support caused Lan's "headaches". If Lan's teacher can give her more support make her to familiar with the new classroom interaction types, her "headaches" can be cured earlier without leaving "scars" for her future learning. Unlike Lan, Ling's WTC increases if the teacher is "fair" to her, resulting from her past experience of being discriminated against by an English teacher. Besides, an introvert personality and positive expectation of evaluation plays additional roles to hinder Ling's WTC.

8.2 Stimulated recalls

Table 20

Students' SR of willingness to communicate classroom interactions

Number	Name	Type of an interaction						Classroom context
		T-S			S-S			
		T-C	T-G	T-I	I-C	I-G	I-I	
S1	Lan				b	*		supportive
S2	Lai				b	*		supportive

Continued

Number	Name	Type of an interaction						Classroom context
		T-S			S-S			
		T-C	T-G	T-I	I-C	I-G	I-I	
S3	Ni			*		a	a	weak
S4	Huang					a	a	weak
S5	Ling			*	*			supportive
S6	Jing				*	a	*	supportive
S7	Bing	*			b	a		weak
S8	Bin	*			b			weak
S9	Lu					a	*	weak
S10	Zhou					a	*	weak
S11	Xiao					a	a	weak
S12	Yu	*						weak
Total count		3	0	2	6	9	6	

Note: * = the teacher used this type of interaction; a = the teacher did not use this type of interaction; b = the teacher used this type of interaction before but not in this observed class.

After classroom observations, twelve stimulated recalls of the observed classrooms conducted respectively with each of the twelve student participants. According to Table 20, it was found that the types of classroom interactions that the students liked differed from what was actually carried out by the teachers, especially those in the weak classroom contexts. In English lessons, most students liked group work, followed by other interactions between students, such as presentation and pair work, instead of other interactions with the teacher. But in fact, group work and pair work were employed by far few teachers than their students expected. Interestingly, no interviewed student mentioned the interaction type between the English teacher and a group of BE students.

8.3 *Student interviews*

Twelve semi-structured interviews were conducted with the twelve BE students to find out the personal factors hinder or enable students' WTC in spoken English. Semi-structured interview questions can be referred to in Appendix D. For instance, after a student answers the pre-specified question of "with whom do you feel most comfortable to communicate", further questions will be followed to probe into "why with that person(s) you feel most comfortable to communicate". Interviews of the four categories of students were coded thematically according to the sub-factors in Chinese WTC model. Categories One and Three each has four BE students while Categories Two and Four each has only two BE students. Except Ling, all BE students desire to communicate in spoken English. Ling has no interest in learning English and the reason she is here pursuing the BE degree despite her dislike of English is that she needed to obey her parents' decision.

Figure 21 shows how many students in each category are influenced by the eight WTC factors. On the whole, students all have group cohesiveness and affiliation. The next factor that was mentioned most by BE students is positive expectation of evaluation, which eleven BE students reported. The factors followed are task-orientation and inhibited monitor, with ten

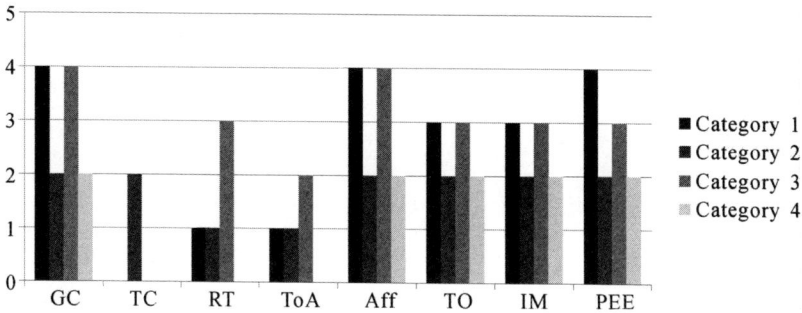

Figure 21. Numbers of the four categories of BE students influenced by WTC factors.

Note:

GC=group cohesiveness,　TC=teacher support,

RT=risk-taking,　　　　　ToA=tolerance of ambiguity,

Aff=affiliation,　　　　　TO=task-orientation,

IM=inhibited monitor,

PEE=positive expectation of evaluation;

Category 1=high WTC+weak classroom context,

Category 2=high WTC+supportive classroom context,

Category 3=low WTC+weak classroom context,

Category 4=low WTC+supportive classroom context.

students reporting that they were under their influence. The least reported factor is good teacher support, which only two BE students in the second category of high WTC and supportive classroom context reported receiving.

　　A special case is that the number of Category 3 students who mentioned risk-taking, tolerance of ambiguity in classroom English learning exceeds the number of students in the other three categories. Only two high WTC students and one each in categories one and two reported they would like to take risks in the spoken English learning process. The same situation happened in respect of tolerance of ambiguity. The following sections will describe these influential WTC factors in detail with selected representative sample excerpts from student interview transcripts.

8.3.1 *Societal context*

With regard to societal context, BE students all reported group cohesiveness while only two high WTC students in the supportive classroom context reported good teacher support. For one thing, students with no matter high or low WTC in both BEE and BBE programmes, all show a preference for sitting with acquaintances rather than with people who were not very familiar or intimate in the English classrooms. For example, Jing said, "I have already formed the habit, because from year one to year three I always sit like this." (S6) The students in a group consist largely of roommates and some others of good friends. In China, it is required that undergraduates should all live at campus. Thus, students spend more time with roommates or good friends not only in lessons but also after class. Students were willing to communicate in pairs or groups with familiar people, as they felt to be "freer" to speak out in such interactions.

"I am very willing to do this ... It doesn't matter even if I make a mistake ... It won't be that you have to intentionally to check this word, then will be more willing to speak ... As to not very familiar (people), I feel very timid." (Ex. 1: S7)

"That feeling is much more familiar ... (I) feel that being with relatively familiar people is relatively freer, relatively opener ..." (Ex. 2: S5)

For another thing, the teacher support result is the same as what we found in student narratives. The students in the weak classroom contexts reported little teacher support. Meanwhile, even in supportive classroom contexts, the two low WTC BE students referred to the imbalance between their needs in spoken English learning and teacher support. Of the students who mention the lack of support from teachers, Ni, for example, said there were limited chances of speaking English in classroom and teacher's nomination of students sometimes decreased her WTC when she came across something that she couldn't answer. Also, the teacher is the last person that she usually turns to for help.

"Our class is generally relatively introvert; most often the teacher nominates students to answer questions. Just like this ... What I know I will happy to say, but for something I am not very clear about, if the teacher forces me to say, that feeling is the worst ... Not very often, if sometimes no one can solve the problem, we will ask the teacher." (Ex. 3: S7)

On the contrary, instructions of the two high WTC students' teachers facilitated the two students' WTC. Innovative and diverse forms of interactions were carried out to support the two students. For instance, Lai mentioned the English teacher increased his WTC and he really admired his teacher's competence to conduct various and "many" interactions in the English classroom.

"As to interactions, the interactions between the teacher and us are many. Sometimes I don't even know what she wants to do. She just sometimes thinks up some ideas ... I can't think of her ideas ... " (Ex. 4: S10)

8.3.2 Personality

As to personality, in total, only five interviewees reported their risk-taking while just four students raised tolerance of ambiguity in their English classrooms. That means nearly two thirds of the students addressed the avoidance of risk-taking and tolerance of ambiguity in the personality factor. With regard to risk-taking, for instance, Ni suggested her introvert personality led to her being unwilling to take risks. She refused to speak in English if she didn't have "full preparation". Even if she was ready to speak, she hesitated and didn't dare to be "the first one to say" in the English classroom.

"My personality tends to be relatively introverted ... it means if I have full preparation, I will. If I feel that I have no idea about it, I won't. I like to prepare in advance ... I will first look around, (to see) if anyone knows, and I won't pop out as the first one to say ... " (Ex. 5: S7)

Considering tolerance of ambiguity, while asking whether they would try their best or would not try to know an unknown language point in a spoken task, two thirds of the students responded they would. As Ni and Bin pointed out, this kind of intolerance of ambiguity action was out of students' language focus on vocabulary and grammar learning and exam-orientation, probably resulting from the traditional audio-lingual way of learning.

"Yes, I am and will be focused on vocabulary and grammar. So usually I will study a grammatical point till I fully understand it. " (Ex. 6: S7)

"Yes, sure, that needs to be understood. If I don't know,

how to do it when it appears on the test paper?" (Ex. 7: S4)

Surprisingly, three out of four students in the third category of low WTC and weak classroom context mentioned that they tended to be risk-taking and it was two out of four in tolerance of ambiguity, whereas no students in the second category of low WTC and supportive classroom context put them forward, and similarly merely one out of four high WTC students in Category One and one out of two high WTC participants in Category Two advanced the two factors. Comparing the interview transcripts of these students, it was found that the high WTC students were competent English learners with self-confidence to be risk-taking and tolerant of ambiguity. In contrast, it is a puzzle that these low WTC students, though without high perceived communication competence, were risk-taking and tolerant of ambiguity. Yu for instance, unlike those students who were unwilling to take risks, initiated questions inside the English classroom directly to ask the teacher instead of quietly consulting the classmates in the lesson or asking the teacher after the class. Also, he would "pass" the relatively unimportant things while performing spoken tasks due to his laziness.

"Ask the teacher ah, what the main idea is, just always ask, just directly when in the classroom... Maybe relatively not so important; may just pass it, just relatively lazy for a while, just don't want to study it. "(Ex. 8: S12)

Further studies can be conducted to explore this phenomenon.

8.3.3 *Motivation*

Affiliation and task-orientation are the components of

motivation in the Chinese WTC model. BE students all agreed that they had affiliation with a certain group. This certain group as suggested in the cohesiveness part, were most often roommates, or some good friends, with whom they sat together in the English classroom. For instance, Zhou felt most relaxed while speaking to his desk mate. Similarly, Xiao figured out the formation of having affiliation to a particular group in the English classroom resulted from those classmates with whom he had more contacts in campus life, possessing the same goal in English learning as well as the teacher's tacit permission of having such a group. In this case, the attachment to a certain group intrigued their willingness to communicate.

"Just those at ordinary times relatively play more together... I will ask the boy next to me, because he is relatively nice. " (Ex. 9: S2)

"I have a relatively fixed one, just one, because we just have the same goal, often eat together and just sit together to say, just relatively close... Then the teacher does not deliberately say you have to (sit) separately ... " (Ex. 10: S11)

Ten out of twelve students mentioned task-orientation in the English classroom. The Chinese conceptualization of WTC suggested by Wen and Clément (2003) described in the literature review chapter noted that task-orientation related to the rationale of establishing one's perceived communication competence not only on one's own judgment but also on the others'. For instance, Jing, with high WTC, put forward the influences of both others and herself to her perceived communication competence.

"I think that both ways, as to the first aspect, although

maybe you think that your spoken English is quite fluent, just go out or to say in some contests compete with others, you will know, actually you are not good ... But your self-consciousness should always warn yourself, just to say that you still have huge improvement room waiting for you ... " (Ex. 11: S6)

Also, task-orientation consists of anxiety and perceived communication competence, which is associated with self-confidence. The ten students though suggested having task-orientation, the extents of the influences of the others and of themselves on the students were various. Emphasizing the influence of the others, for example, Ni's self-confidence was highly decreased, since she often received negative feedback from her teacher. This largely destroyed her willingness to communicate in the English classroom. Focusing on the influence of oneself, for instance, Bing contributed her anxious feeling when she cannot answer a question to her insufficient learning.

"Just the feeling that after I say something, the teacher will correct my pronunciation, then I feel it still not good ... Usually when I answer, the teacher will say something and give me some little feedbacks so (I) will think I still have no improvement. " (Ex. 12: S7)

"If I don't know the answer, I will surely be nervous ... I don't study enough ... " (Ex. 13: S3)

As to the two students who said they had no task-orientation, one student Bin was very confident with his spoken English, due to the experience he gained from spoken English contests; distinctly, the other student, (although he did not have high perceived communication competence), Yu was not anxious in the classroom interactions.

"When answering questions I'm relatively relaxed ... If I don't know, I will say I have no idea... In the past I felt nervous; now after joining some competitions I get some experience." (Ex. 14: S4)

"If I initiate the answer I will surely not be nervous. It surely is that I know the answer if I am called, if I know (the answer) I won't be nervous, and I just answer." (Ex. 15: S12)

8.3.4 *Attitudes*

Attitudes are composed of an inhibited monitor and positive expectation of evaluation. Ten BE students addressed the inhibited monitor, expressing in the lower competence they perceived they had, the more correction they would like to have. Taking Xiao for instance, she thought her communication competence was "just so so" and expressed "heartache feeling" if she couldn't find the correct answer to an unknown language point.

"(My spoken English) is just so so... (as to a language problem) I will first ask classmates next to me, then if it doesn't work, I will ask the teacher after the class, because if I encounter something and don't explore it, I will have the heartache feeling."(Ex. 16: S11)

Other four students tended not to possess an inhibited monitor. For instance, Lu, who had high perceived communication competence, refused to attend to the final correct grammatical form when doing a spoken English task. Instead, she would like to use another way of expressing herself to get her meaning across. In the second half of his interview Excerpt Eight cited about the tolerance of ambiguity in the personalty section,

Yu (who has low WTC) showed he did not correct more while having lower perceived communication competence, as he was too lazy to find the correct answer.

"For example, if just we two are talking in English, we should express our ideas clearly. If we think the grammar is difficult, just express in another way. " (Ex. 17: S1)

With regard to positive expectations of evaluation, nine BE students mentioned it. Yu was the exception. For instance, Ni expected to obtain positive evaluation from her classmates and the teacher in English classrooms with the wish of her ideas being "recognized" by the others. Similarly, Huang was afraid of getting negative "confused" evaluation from the others, which would make him feel "awkward".

"I relatively care about the reactions of the others. I relatively like the others to recognize me. " (Ex. 18: S7)

"If I use an inappropriate word, it will make others confused. Then I will speak very carefully. If I still make a mistake, it will be awkward. "(Ex. 19: S8)

Yu is unique in this case as not expecting positive evaluation from others, which may be because of his personality—he does not consider much about others' thoughts.

"As to me, I won't consider much about what others think. " (Ex. 20: S12)

8. 4 *Discussion*

The discussion will focus on the vertical codes of the eight sub-factors (group cohesiveness, teacher support, risk-taking, tolerance of ambiguity, affiliation, task-orientation, inhibited monitor and positive expectation of evaluation) of Chinese conceptualization of L2 WTC in classrooms and horizontal codes of high and low WTC in the weak and supportive contexts to answer the three research questions at the personal level. At present, a good language learner is constructed both by the individual self and via communication with the targeted community (Norton &. Toohey, 2001). Thus, excerpts mentioning contextual factors, personal contexts need to be covered. In addition, when integrating findings from Studies One and Two to discuss more issues in this chapter, a discrepancy between quantitative and qualitative outcomes emerges.

8.4.1 Research Question One—personal factors that facilitate or hinder BE students' WTC

The first research question of what personal factors hinder or enable individual BE students' WTC in spoken English in English classrooms can be answered through revisiting the four categories of WTC student participants' perspectives about the eight sub-factors of L2 WTC (Wen &. Clément, 2003). Group cohesiveness and affiliation can in some circumstances facilitate students' WTC, whereas insufficient teacher support, unwillingness to take risks, intolerance of ambiguity, task-orientation, inhibited monitor and positive expectation of evaluation hinder students' WTC. An exception is found in the second category of WTC students with high WTC and supportive classroom contexts: They receive enough teacher support in English lessons, which enables their WTC.

8.4.1.1 Two factors enable WTC

To begin with, the four categories of WTC students all reported group cohesiveness and affiliation, which can facilitate participants' spoken English learning. This finding disagrees with Wen and Clément's (2003) Chinese L2 WTC model. Wen and Clément regard group cohesiveness and affiliation as two factors, associated with each other, which Chinese learners of English have to overcome in classroom learning. Eye contact, for example, can be associated with affiliative motivation, as the approach or avoidance of eye contact expresses the physical distance and the level of intimacy between two or more persons (Argyle & Dean, 1965). However, cohesiveness and affiliation in a certain group cannot hinder students' WTC in all conditions for all Chinese learners of English.

With the goal of affiliation, it is possible to increase unconscious mimicry (Lakin & Chartrand, 2003). According to Lankin and Chartrand, unconscious mimicry of a person who engages in a L2 learning behavior can make the perceiver concentrate more on the same behavior. Furthermore, the more unsuccessful one is in trying to affiliate in an interaction, the more mimicry one would exhibit. In this sense, if all group members act with the same goal of improving spoken English with high WTC, one is able to have increased unconscious mimicry to perform the same targeted movement and thus it is possible to have one's level of spoken English raised.

8.4.1.2 Six factors hinder WTC

Nevertheless, other than group cohesiveness and affiliation, the six factors hindered BE students' WTC and this is consistent with

Wen and Clément's（2003）Chinese WTC conceptualization. For instance, only two students in the second category of high WTC and supportive classroom context reported teacher support and thus more teacher support needs to be provided to students in order to facilitate their enhancement of WTC. Likewise, student narratives showed that no matter whether they experienced weak or supportive English lessons in the past, currently, only the two students in the second category were satisfied with classroom contexts. For the other three categories of students, the present teacher support was insufficient for them. For example, speaking chances in lessons is an issue that produced complaints or praise from students. Also, stimulated recall results stated students' preferences for a student-centered approach to English learning in lessons. However, there was a discrepancy between student expectation and teacher instructions. For instance, students wanted more group work and pair work than was actually carried out by teachers. In this case, the teacher can consider setting up more group and pair work in English lessons to fulfill students' communicative needs.

Now, the other five sub-factors of WTC will be further explained. Firstly, the low amount of risk-taking and tolerance of ambiguity unveiled in this study confirmed Wen and Clément's（2003）theoretical assumption towards Chinese learners of English in the classroom context, indicating that BE students were afraid of making mistakes and then losing face in front of the others. The low level of risk-taking result is also consistent with Liu and Jackson's（2008）study outcome. Their study concerned students' hindrances in risk-taking, anxiety and fear of negative evaluations in L2 learning, which were quite congruent with what was found in this WTC study.

Secondly, the majority of BE students linked task-orientation with anxiety and low perceived communication competence in spoken English, which hindered their WTC in English classrooms. Similar findings can be found in Liu's (2006) and Liu and Jackson's (2008) studies. They suggested that Chinese students' unwillingness to communicate and anxiety correlated significantly. More research outcomes also discovered perceived communication competence and anxiety were correlated with L2 WTC (MacIntyre & Doucette, 2010; Peng & Woodrow, 2010). The motivation factor includes the above-mentioned affiliation. It is noted in the literature review chapter that task-orientation is related with perceived communication competence and anxiety. Self-confidence can be examined through perceived communication competence and anxiety (Centinkaya, 2005) and the high self-confidence can raise motivation (Dörnyei, 2001).

Thirdly, most students mentioned inhibited monitor and positive expectation of evaluation, implying they had hindrances in the attitude factor. Without doubt, an inhibited monitor can hinder the attitude process and cause side-effects to students' WTC. Moreover, in line with this study, Liu and Jackson's (2008) unwillingness to communicate study found fear of getting negative evaluations among Chinese L2 learning students, which was expressed in their unwillingness to conduct public-speaking and exam-taking.

8. 4. 2   *Research Question Three — interactions between personal and contextual factors*

The third research question of how these factors interact

with each other to influence BE students' WTC in spoken English in English lessons can be answered by re-using the last chapter mentioned Cao's (2011) three dimensions of contextual WTC under the ecological perspective. Of the three environmental, individual and linguistic dimensions, Study Three falls into the individual/personal aspects (i. e. perceived opportunity to communicate, personality, self-confidence and emotion) and linguistic aspects (i. e. language proficiency).

Among the eight sub-factors of WTC, students' attachment to group members to some extent enhanced their affiliative motivation in English learning, leading to the increase of WTC. However, inadequate teacher support, risk-taking and tolerance of ambiguity as well as excessive task-orientation, inhibited monitor and positive expectation of evaluation indeed affected each other and might decrease students' WTC. Without a supportive context constructed by teachers, a student might not be able to move forward language-learning without being anxious or bored (Freeman & Freeman, 2004). Also, taking risks of having errors in a non-threatening interaction environment can provoke a student's potential in language learning (Richard-Amato, 2003). Conversely, the few number of student participants suggested risk-taking and tolerance of ambiguity in the four categories of WTC can hinder students' L2 learning and WTC.

Moreover, this study supports the findings of Ma, Zhang and Hu (2004) and Yu (2011): Optimistic motivation and attitudes were found to be positively related with WTC for Chinese learners of English. It can be assumed that many low perceived communication competence mentioned by participants resulted in high amount of inhibited monitor (Wen & Clément, 2003). Meanwhile, lots of students had positive expectation of evaluation from teachers and peers, which was out of the face-protection approach (Dörnyei, 2001).

8.4.3 Research Question Four—pedagogical changes

8.4.3.1 Sufficient use of codeswitching

More pedagogical suggestions are proposed for answering the fourth research question to supplement those in Chapter Seven. To start with, narrative results especially, showed students' need for fair and more provision of speaking chances in English classrooms while referring to their WTC in spoken English. Despite utilizing attainable, authentic but challenging tasks congruent with the Chinese culture to adjust task difficulty, the sufficient use of codeswitching can also tune up task difficulty and create more speaking opportunities for students. An element building supportive classroom environment is to use codeswitching with the intertwined application of L1 and L2 (Cook, 2001; Liebscher & Dailey-O'Cain, 2005), making task difficulty linguistically at an acceptable level for BE students. Codeswitching aims to be functional in L2 classroom and it is defined as a "communicative resource which enables teachers and students to accomplish a considerable range of social and educational objectives" (Adendorff, 1996, p. 389). The norm of using no native language other than second language in codeswitching is widely agreed with the preference of immersion mode (Rolin-Ianziti & Brownlie, 2002; Macaro, 2001); nevertheless, opponents of the view tend to be against the pure L2 language mode in classroom settings and back up the use of L1 in classroom with the consideration of individual teacher preference differences (Levine, 2003; Jørgensen, 2005; van der Meij & Zhao, 2010).

Teachers and BE students' views on the teachers' codeswitching frequency in China was studied, showing that both teachers and students thought that codeswitching is desirable and functional in the classroom environment (van der Meij & Zhao, 2010); however, there was a large distance from what the teachers believed in and what BE students actually needed. That is, although teachers employed seven times more frequent and ten times longer switches than they believed, BE students in reality desired more and longer switches. Guo (2007) calls for written policies regulating codeswitching in schools in China while pointing out the omission of the codeswitching issue in 2001 and 2004's new syllabi designed by the Ministry of Education. In this sense, with sufficient use of switches, English classroom teachers can provide more attainable tasks for BE students.

8.4.3.2　*More S-S than T-S interactions*

Secondly, consistent with the suggestion noted in Chapter Six, more S-S interactions than T-S interactions can be used by teachers to form a less-threatening environment for students (Paulsen, Bru & Murberg, 2006). Kraft (1985) claimed that students could experience evaluation better in small groups instead of the whole class, making passive students more willing to communicate in classrooms. Stimulated recalls results of willing to communicate interaction types also found that BE students tended to prefer S-S interactions to T-S interactions. Meanwhile, relating to student interviews, group cohesiveness and affiliation were discovered to be able to support BE students'

L2 learning. This insider effect phenomenon among BE students is out of collective Chinese culture (Wen & Clément, 2003). Hu (2002) argued that collaborative learning, in this study for instance, S-S interactions such as pair and group work can match the Chinese culture of learning, making students more relaxed and willing to speak in English classrooms just as they referred to the feeling of conducting pair or group work in class.

8.4.3.3 Strategies for improving motivation and attitudes

Thirdly, student interview results showed that, most students had problems in risk-taking and tolerance of ambiguity in the personality factor, motivational factors such as task-orientation on perceived communication competence and anxiety, inhibited monitor and positive expectation of evaluation in the attitude factor as well as teacher support. Since a student's personality can be influenced by motivation and attitudes in the Chinese WTC model (Wen & Clément, 2003), strategies suggested for minimizing hindrances in motivation and attitudes, then can be applied to make students more risk-taking and tolerant of ambiguity.

Teachers can help students set more learning goals to turn their task-orientation to task-mastery in speaking (Schunk, 1996). According to Schunk, the goal that a student seeks in L2 learning can be a learning goal or a performance goal or a combined learning and performance goal, which is related with motivation. In this case, with a learning goal, the ultimate outcome is to gain academic achievement via the development of the speaking skill. Task-mastery strategies are employed, and students' self-efficacy, motivation and self-regulation can be raised in the process. Distinctly, a performance goal is analogous to task-orientation. With a performance goal, one's ability is assessed through parallel comparison of their task completion with the others in the society. However, such social comparisons can make students have low perceived competence while facing difficult tasks and this will affect their task motivation (Ames, 1992; Jagacinski, 1992). A combined learning and performance goal can be established when students have to learn the skill and finish lots of works. Therefore, teachers can assist BE students to establish more learning goals and making them more confident in their spoken English.

Furthermore, teachers can provide constant guided-feedbacks to BE students to reduce their WTC hindrances in anxiety and attitudes such as inhibited monitor and positive expectation of evaluation. Hyland (2003) found that the two interviewed students from Taiwan in a Hong Kong university cared much about teacher feedback, which influenced their motivation and attitudes in English writing. The same perspective can be applied to the speaking context; as in China, teacher feedback is suggested as vital for students' English learning at the tertiary level (Liu & Li, 2005). Instead of directly pointing out students' mistakes in spoken English, students prefer discrete feedback from the teacher and thus it seems more proper to use indirect feedback (Ge & Gao, 2005; Yu, 2010). Yu proposed for easing students' anxiety, the teacher could first encourage the student with praise, and then guide the student to find the errors. In this sense, students can both receive positive evaluation from the teacher and not be too inhibited to overcorrect mistakes. The next chapter will combine data of the three studies and discuss some key issues.

Chapter 9
Discussion

This chapter will discuss findings from the three studies. Findings are presented in a three-dimension Chinese L2 WTC pyramid model. Quantitative and qualitative data are combined and inconsistent findings of the kinds of data in Studies One and Three are discussed. Findings are then compared with previous L2 WTC studies. Finally, the lack of teacher support issue will be discussed.

9.1 Combining findings

9.1.1 A three-dimension Chinese L2 WTC model

Integrating the findings of the three studies, a Chinese L2 WTC model with linguistic, individual and contextual dimensions is proposed in Figure 22. The pyramid model shows that the bottom six layers of personality, DC, attitudes, motivation, societal context and the linguistic aspect overlaps to influence Chinese BE students' L2 WTC. The contextual aspect includes DC, societal context (teacher support & group cohesiveness), motivation (affiliation & task-orientation) and attitudes (inhibited monitor & positive expectation of evaluation). The individual aspect consists of DC, factors in motivation and attitudes as well as personality (risk-taking & tolerance of ambiguity). The linguistic aspect is comprised of language proficiency. In this study it is BE students' spoken English proficiency in English lessons.

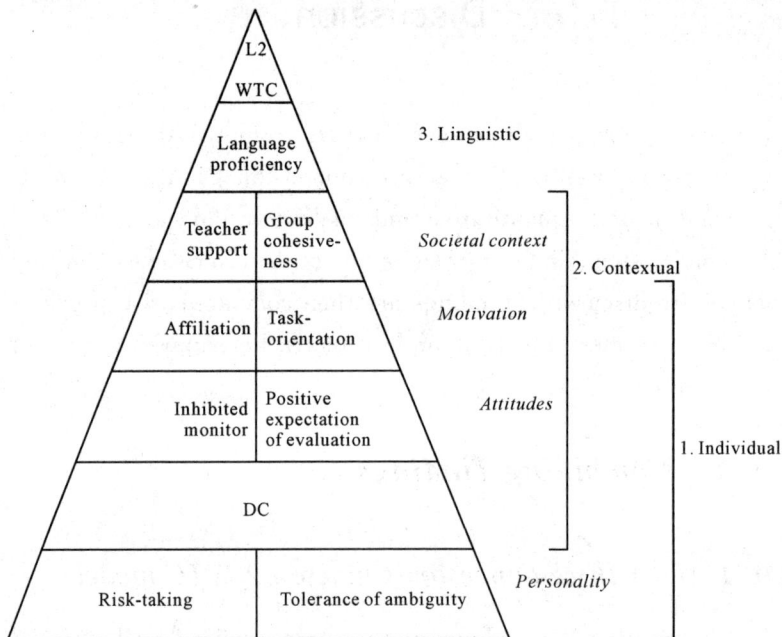

Figure 22. A three-dimension Chinese L2 WTC model in English lessons.

Figure 22 was built based on Figure 23 and Figure 24. Drawing on Cao's (2011) three dimensions of contextual WTC from the ecological perspective, Studies Two and Three researched how personal and contextual WTC factors interacted within the environmental, personal and linguistic aspects. Study

Two explored the environmental (i. e. topic, task type, interlocutor, teacher and class interactional pattern) and linguistic aspects (i. e. language proficiency). In this case, suitable interaction types and attainable task difficulty are environmentally and linguistically established for BE students can increase students' WTC. Study Three found the individual/ personal (i. e. perceived opportunity to communicate, personality, self-confidence and emotion) and linguistic aspects (i. e. language proficiency). Different from previous scale studies in L1 WTC, L2 WTC theories and studies have been developing to include not only scales, but also qualitative and mixed methods studies since the introduction of MacIntyre et al. 's (1998) L2 WTC pyramid model. L2 WTC includes both trait and contextual features. A student can have a certain level of trait-like WTC, but the level of WTC can be fluctuated in different contexts.

Figure 23 answers Research Question One about which personal factors hindered or enabled BE students' WTC in speaking in English language lessons. The pyramid figure includes linguistic and individual domains. The linguistic domain consists of language proficiency in spoken English. The individual domain consists of DC and factors in motivation (affiliation & task-orientation) as well as attitudes (inhibited monitor & positive expectation of evaluation) and personality (risk-taking & tolerance of ambiguity).

Contextual factors that hindered or enabled BE students' WTC in speaking in English language lessons can be answered by Figure 24. The pyramid figure includes linguistic and contextual domains. The linguistic domain consists of language proficiency

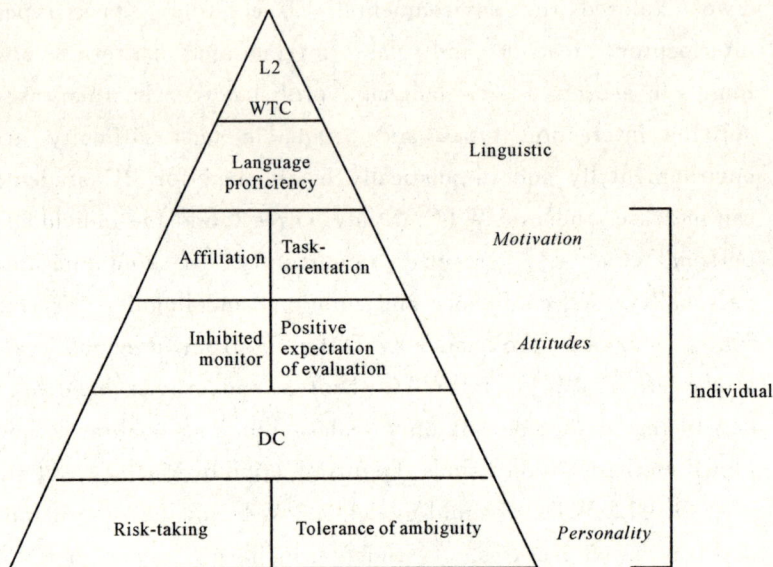

Figure 23. Personal factors influence BE students' WTC.

in spoken English. The contextual domain consists of DC and factors in motivation (affiliation & task-orientation) as well as attitudes (inhibited monitor & positive expectation of evaluation) and societal context (teacher support & group cohesiveness).

9.1.2   *Data combining outcomes*

Since qualitative data in Studies Two and Three were already converted into quantitative data, it was time to compare these transformed quantitative data with quantitative data in Study One. The comparing outcome was that the factors hindering BE students' WTC were DC, societal context (group cohesiveness & teacher support), motivation (affiliation & perceived communication competence in task-orientation), and

206

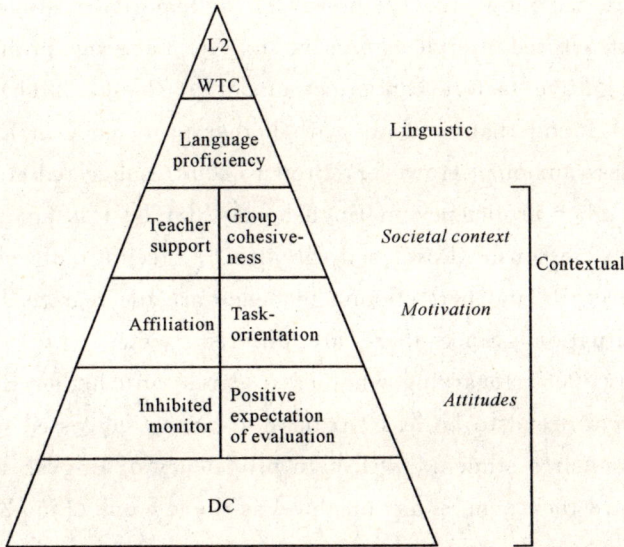

Figure 24. Contextual factors influence BE students' WTC.

attitudes （inhibited monitor ＆ positive expectation of evaluation） and personality （risk-taking ＆ tolerance of ambiguity）. The factors that facilitate BE students' WTC were language proficiency and low anxiety.

Study Two explores contextual factors while Studies One and Three asked for personal factors. Different findings emerged in Study One and Study Three. Study One suggested that among the investigated variables of WTC, only low anxiety enabled BE students' WTC in speaking in English lessons. In contrast, Study Three found that DC, group cohesiveness and affiliation rather than anxiety enabled BE students' WTC.

To begin with, apparently contradicting findings of anxiety level appear in questionnaires in Study One and student interviews in Study Three. Questionnaires show that BE students have low anxiety; however, the majority of students in semi-structured interviews present anxiety. Language proficiency and cognitive factors can affect anxiety (Zhang, 2011). Liu (2006) found that students with higher proficiency in English were less anxious. However, Brown (2008) suggested students with higher proficiency in English may not be less anxious in English lessons. Low self-confidence, feeling of shame, inferiority or/and perfectionist tendency are the reasons behind this situation. Since there are different views (Liu, 2006; Brown, 2008) regarding whether students with higher English proficiency tend to be less anxious, it can be suggested that in questionnaires students with high proficiency of English tended to regard their general anxious level as the low one (Liu, 2006); nevertheless, in real classrooms, students felt that they were anxious in specifically referred task situations out of the perfectionist tendency (Brown, 2008).

Another different finding between Study One and Study Three was in DC, group cohesiveness and affiliation. Eleven out of twelve interviewees reported DC (desire to communicate with a specific person or persons) and all of them suggested group cohesiveness and affiliation could enable their spoken English learning and provoke WTC in the classroom; nonetheless, only moderate level of DC, group cohesiveness and affiliation were presented in the questionnaires in Study One.

9.2 Relating findings with previous L2 WTC studies

The findings of the three studies modified Wen and

Clément's （2003） Chinese conceptualization of L2 WTC in English classrooms. The factors that facilitated and hindered BE students' WTC in spoken English in English lessons were mostly in consistent with pervious L2 WTC studies and Wen and Clément's (2003) model, except anxiety. The finding of the low anxiety in questionnaires supported Garrott's (1995) and Shi's (2006) studies and challenged the collectivistic outlook of the Chinese due to the influence of globalization. However, anxiety in qualitative studies cannot be regarded as a hindrance for all BE students since only twelve BE students were studied. The finding of anxiety among higher proficiency BE students in qualitative studies seemed to support Brown's （2008） perfectionist tendency.

In line with previous L2 WTC studies, the factors facilitated students' WTC were 1) language proficiency（for academically better performing students）(MacIntyre et al. , 1998) and 2) the low anxiety（found in questionnaires）in task-orientation. The factors that hindered students' WTC were 1) DC （Wu &.Wen, 2009), 2) societal context（group cohesiveness （Fushino, 2010; MacIntyre et al. ,2002; Wu &. Wen, 2009) &. teacher support (Peng &. Woodrow, 2010; Wu &. Wen, 2009; Yu, 2011)), 3) motivation（affiliation （Fushino, 2010; MacIntyre et al. ,2002; Wu &.Wen, 2009) &. perceived communication competence (MacIntyre &. Doucette, 2010; Peng, 2008; Peng &. Woodrow, 2010; Wu, 2008) in task-orientation), and 4) attitudes（inhibited monitor （MacIntyre &. Doucette, 2010; Peng, 2008; Peng &. Woodrow, 2010; Wu, 2008) &. positive expectation of evaluation (Wu &. Wen, 2009)) and personality （risk-taking （Wu &. Wen, 2009) &. tolerance of ambiguity （Wen &. Clément, 2003)).

9.3 *Lack of teacher support*

A three-dimension Chinese L2 WTC model (see Figure 22) modified Wen and Clément's (2003) Chinese conceptualization of L2 WTC in English classrooms. For instance, Chinese learners of English tended to have WTC with optimistic motivation and attitudes (Ma, Zhang & Hu, 2004; Yu, 2011). Teachers thus need to help individual BE students to prevent emotional turmoil that can deteriorate their WTC.

However, special attention needs to be paid to the lack of teacher support situation. Quite a few students, of just two students in the second category (of high WTC and supportive classroom context) among the total twelve student participants in their narratives and semi-structured interviews praised present classroom experience as an outcome of sufficient support from teachers in Study Three.

For instance, an issue regarding group work comes up and it seems to be essential to put forward it. Group work is the interaction type that is neglected by teachers in classroom observations in Study Two; however, BE students' stimulated recalls in Study Three after the classes suggested it is their preferred communicative interaction type in English lessons. Liu's (2006) study outcome supports the application of group work since the least anxious environment is conducting group and pair work in English lessons.

For students in Category One of high WTC and weak classroom context, Study Two came up with some pedagogical recommendations, concerning curriculum development and task interaction types and difficulty adjustment. First of all, teachers and course designers should pay more attention to curriculum development, since it is an essential element guiding classroom instructions, especially for students in the direction of Business English, their instrumental motivation to learn English is different from those students in English Education due to their different future career orientations. Secondly, though high WTC students demonstrated their preferences to conduct easy tasks, it may damage students' speaking skill development in the long run. Teachers thus need to help them develop skills through the use of authentic, attainable but challenging tasks consistent with Chinese culture, for instance, some strategies suggested by Moon can be learned to facilitate students' WTC in the classroom. Thirdly, some students seemed to be unwilling to cooperate with the teacher such as in Lin's situation. In this case, potential rewarding strategies can be brought in, such as the eleven prosocial behavior alteration techniques (BATs) (Paulsel, 2004:45): "Immediate reward from behavior, deferred reward, reward from others, self-esteem, responsibility to class, normative rules, altruism, peer modeling, teacher modeling, expert teacher, and teacher feedback.". However, Kearney et al. (1984) claimed the effective application of these strategies can be restrained by lack of judgment on specific contexts, teaching experiences and teachers' reflections.

As to Category Four of low WTC and supportive classroom context, Studies One and Three put forward sufficient use of codeswitching, experience evaluation in more S-S interactions than T-S interactions, learning goals setting for task-mastery, and constant guided feedbacks.

A series of studies supports the pedagogical implications suggested in this study. To start with, codeswitching between L1 and L2 is desirable and functional for Chinese learners of English; nonetheless, there is a distance from teachers' beliefs (seven times more frequent and ten times longer switches) and students' real needs of more and longer switches (van der Meij & Zhao, 2010). Proper application of code-switches can linguistically tune-up task difficulty and create more speaking chances for individual BE student. Next, Hu (2002) points out that collaborative learning is congruent with the Chinese culture of learning, since students reports the feeling of being more relaxed and have higher WTC in pair and group works in classroom settings. More interactions among students rather than the interaction between the teacher and the students can be considered to make students experiences evaluation in less-threatening environments such as small group work rather than the whole class (Paulsen, Bru & Murberg, 2006). Then, besides the two strategies for improving teacher support, ways to make a change to students' motivation and attitudes can be employed. Teachers can both help students establish learning goals for task-mastery to minimize hindrances in motivation and attitudes and constantly provide feedbacks to students to reduce their anxiety and develop positive attitudes. In addition, for students in the third category of low WTC and weak classroom context, the teacher can apply all the recommendations suggested above.

Chapter 10
Conclusions

10. 1   Research mission of the study

The central mission of this Chinese WTC project is to solve the research problem of why many Bachelor of English (BE) students seem not to be willing to speak in English classrooms in China, in spite of the nationwide need and awareness of learning English as a second language at the tertiary level along with the globalization process. The investigation was motivated by the confusion from my past teaching experience as an English teacher in China and the interest in exploring BE students' WTC in the Chinese culture after the education reform of cultivating inter-disciplinary English such as English Education and Business English, instead of the single linguistic subject for English students (ELT Advisory Board under the Ministry of Education, 2000).

The contribution of this book lies in finding the problems behind students' lack of WTC for classroom teachers who are instructing BE students in China. Strategies, such as providing more opportunities to communicate, carrying out challenging but attainable tasks, using authentic, real-world activities, and

213

giving proper feedback (Rutherford & Ahlgren, 1990) as well as experience evaluation in a less-threatening environment, of small groups instead of the whole class situation (Kraft, 1985), were suggested to enhance the four categories of BE students' WTC (classified by high and low WTC as well as supportive and weak classroom contexts) in spoken English in English classrooms. It is also possible to provide pedagogical changes to spoken English teaching for Chinese students in various classroom contexts across the nation or around the world.

A mixed research methods design with a case study approach aimed to reach the purpose of the study to find out the personal and contextual factors influencing willingness to communicate (WTC) in spoken English in English language classrooms in China. Four research questions were established to resolve the research aim with three sequential and triangulate-analyzed studies. Study One of self-reported questionnaires and Study Three of student narratives, stimulated recalls and semi-structured interviews with students sought to answer three research questions at the personal level: the first research question of what personal factors hindered or enabled individual BE students' spoken English in classrooms; the third research question of how these factors interacted to influence WTC in spoken English in English language classrooms; and the final question of what pedagogical changes could be drawn to enhance BE students' WTC in English classrooms. Study Two of documents, videotaped classroom observations and semi-structured interviews with teachers were used to settle three research questions at the contextual level: The second research question of what contextual factors hindered or enabled BE students' spoken English in classrooms as well as the third and fourth research questions. Based on Wen and Clément's (2003) Chinese conceptualization of WTC in classrooms, the main findings of the book will be stated according to the four research questions.

10.2 *Summary of findings*

Findings of this study suggested a pyramid model for Chinese BE students in the linguistic, individual and contextual dimensions (see Figure 22). The results modified Wen and Clément's (2003) Chinese L2 WTC model. In line with Wen and Clément, the factors that hindered BE students' WTC were language proficiency, DC, societal context (group cohesiveness & teacher support), motivation (affiliation & perceived communication competence in task-orientation), and attitudes (inhibited monitor & positive expectation of evaluation) and personality (risk-taking & tolerance of ambiguity). Different from Wen and Clément's (2003) WTC model presumption of possessing anxiety in task-orientation, BE students tended to have low anxiety in speaking in English lessons.

However, there were discrepancies among the three study findings. Inconsistent findings were found in anxiety in task-orientation. Study One found that students had low anxiety whereas Study Three found that students were anxious while speaking English in lessons. It was further explored that BE students with high proficiency had the perfectionist tendency. Thus, only low anxiety enabled BE students' WTC. Inconsistent findings also emerged in DC, affiliation and group cohesiveness. Study Three found that DC, group cohesiveness and affiliation enabled BE students' WTC, which facilitated their WTC; however, Study One only found moderate levels of DC, group cohesiveness and affiliation. Therefore, BE students had room to improve their DC, group cohesiveness and affiliation.

10.2.1 Research Question One—personal factors that facilitate or hinder BE students' WTC

The first research question asked about what personal factors hinder and facilitate BE students' spoken English in English classrooms. Present Studies One and Three results indicate that BE students are somewhat willing to communicate, for instance, according to the questionnaire outcome, of moderate level. Figure 23 (see Section 9.1.1) shows personal factors that influence BE students' WTC in spoken English in English lessons.

But students have to overcome some hindrances in order to be more willing to communicate. It was agreed by Studies One and Three that the personal factors which hinder BE students' WTC in spoken English in English classrooms can be attributed to five sub-factors in the Chinese WTC conceptualization, of lack of teacher support in the societal context factors, risk-taking and tolerance of ambiguity in the personality factor, as well as inhibited monitor and positive expectation of evaluation in the attitudes factor.

However, there is discrepancy between data from the Study One of quantitative self-reported questionnaires and qualitative data drawn from Study Three. Questionnaires revealed that BE students had low level of anxiety that could facilitate their spoken English learning whereas most student interviewees mentioned anxious feelings in English classrooms (related to task-orientation) hindered their WTC. Those BE students with higher English proficiency tended to perceive their general anxiety level in English lessons were low in questionnaires. Nonetheless, due to the perfectionist tendency, students were anxious to perform tasks in English lessons.

Also, results of students' DC, group cohesiveness and affiliation in Studies One and Three seemed to be different. Study Three suggested that students had DC, group cohesiveness and affiliation; however, Study One suggested that they had moderate levels of DC, group cohesiveness and affiliation. That means BE students had room to improve DC, group cohesiveness and affiliation in order to enhance their WTC.

Unexpectedly, by combining data obtained from cross-validated Study One and Pilot Study Two, structural equation modeling (SEM) in Study One chapter found only one of the seven WTC factors in the model: WTC accounted for merely 5% of BE students' spoken English scores. But the small number cannot be ignored while considering it as an indication of students' improvement in spoken English (MacIntyre et al., 1998). Further multi-group SEM results suggested that different English instructors, programmes and school years tended to be unvaried as to the structural model. In addition, T-test found that year one BE students were different from BE students in the second-and third-years in learning experiences. Compared with the BE freshmen, the BEE sophomores' and juniors' WTC, the level of extrovert personality and perceived communication competence decreased while the BBE sophomores's and juniors'

WTC，DC，affiliation and positive expectation of evaluation lowered.

Study Three chapter further explored individual BE students' WTC by investigating the four categories of WTC BE students. Almost every student, except one student who was forced by her parents to study in the English subject, suggested they had desire to communicate in English classrooms. BE students also mentioned group cohesiveness and affiliation to their roommates or close friends that they often sat together. Stimulated recalls from students suggested that students tended to have higher WTC while interacting with other students rather than with the teacher; for instance, conducting group work is the most willing to communicate interaction type. The lack of teacher support also needs special attention.

10.2.2 *Research Question Two—contextual factors that facilitate or hinder BE students' WTC*

In line with the insufficient teacher support found in research question one at the personal level, the second research question which sought to find more about the contextual factors, especially on faculty and teacher support in study two, came up with the same conclusion. Figure 24 (see Section 9.1.1) shows contextual factors that influence BE students' WTC in spoken English in English lessons.

Study two researched documents, video-taped classroom observations and interviewed one teacher in the supportive classroom context (Moon) and another in the weak context (Lin). Firstly, there was a lack of department support in actual classroom instruction for teachers. For instance, expressed in some apparent missing spoken English curriculum guidelines in documents for students in the direction of Business English and for the juniors and seniors. Secondly, classroom observations found just two out of six teachers demonstrated their classroom instruction that they were supportive for enhancing their students' WTC. Thirdly, two teacher interviews showed that there were indeed differences between teachers' instructions for constructing supportive or weak classroom context.

Study Two also discovered task interaction types and task difficulty affected students' WTC in spoken English. Regarding interaction types and task difficulty, two raters' classroom observation coding outcome found that high and low WTC students were similar in showing the preferences towards student-centered approach such as group work; however, task difficulty had no influence on low WTC students whereas high WTC students preferred conducting easy tasks. High WTC students' attachment to easy tasks is assumed to be out of their afraid of losing face and negative evaluation from others or even perfectionism to avoid burnout in learning (Zhang, Gan & Cham, 2007). In addition, students' WTC as a whole coded from slightly willing to mostly willing, in which high WTC students had more percentages of moderately and mostly willing whereas low WTC had more of slightly willing.

Despite students' inclination to student-centered interactions, teachers would not like to conduct group work in classroom settings. The two teacher interviewees would rather exert their efforts to make their students ready for the national English examination for BE students, TEM 4 or TEM 8. Lin considered it was a temporary moment and should leave group aside for examination preparation while Moon thought it was a complete waste of time to carry out group work in limited classroom time. Besides, unlike Lin's complaints of students' unwillingness to speak owing to their low proficiency in spoken English and lack of enough previous training, Moon utilized some strategies to increase students' WTC, such as a scaffolding way of asking three continuous and related questions, individual student' prepared speech and a two-way discussion afterwards between the speech maker and the other students and between the speech maker and the teacher, as well as his flexible use of textbooks and authentic other relevant materials to facilitate the unit study.

10. 2. 3　*Research Question Three—interactions between personal and contextual factors*

The third research question inquired about interactions between personal and contextual factors influencing WTC. Both trait and contextual WTC studies found the factors in the Chinese conceptualization interacted with each other to affect BE students' WTC. Confirmatory factor analysis (CFA) results showed that the seven measured WTC variables of WTC, DC, personality, affiliation, anxiety, perceived communication competence and positive expectation of evaluation were interrelated with each other, indicating that the Chinese WTC conceptualization proposed by Wen and Clément (2003) indeed affected BE students' WTC in English classroom.

A three-dimension Chinese L2 WTC model (see Figure 22) was then proposed, which include individual, contextual and linguistic aspects based on the findings. The pyramid model shows that the bottom six layers of personality, DC, attitudes, motivation, societal context and the linguistic aspect overlapped to influence Chinese BE students' L2 WTC (see Section 9. 1. 1). The model modified Wen and Clément's (2003) Chinese conceptualization of L2 WTC in English classrooms.

10 . 2. 4   *Research Question Four—pedagogical changes*

The fourth and last research questions sought to find out what pedagogical changes can be drawn to enhance BE students' WTC. A wide range of strategies can be inferred from the four categories of WTC BE students based on the answers from the first three research questions. Teachers should be helpful for BE students in the second category of high WTC and supportive classroom context, and more efforts should be made to improve students' classroom learning experience and their WTC in the other three categories.

Possible implications concerning pedagogical changes for BE students with different WTC and different classroom contexts are presented in Figure 25.

(1) For high WTC students in the first category who are competent and are learning in environments which do not support WTC and pedagogical efforts (e. g. , providing more opportunities to communicate, carrying out challenging but attainable tasks, using authentic, real-world activities, and giving proper feedback—see Rutherford & Ahlgren, 1990 for more details). should be carried out by teachers and universities. For instance, it can be essential to make more teaching materials and textbooks with real world activities to cater for BE students' different future career needs. Thus, students' interests in spoken English can be better stimulated and then lead to their boost of confidence to speak inside English language classrooms.

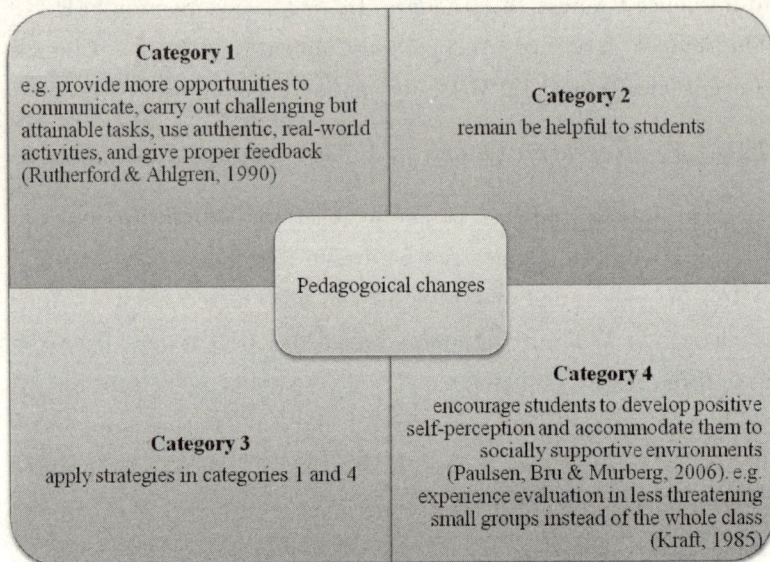

Category 1
e.g. provide more opportunities to communicate, carry out challenging but attainable tasks, use authentic, real-world activities, and give proper feedback (Rutherford & Ahlgren, 1990)

Category 2
remain be helpful to students

Pedagogoical changes

Category 4
encourage students to develop positive self-perception and accommodate them to socially supportive environments (Paulsen, Bru & Murberg, 2006). e.g. experience evaluation in less threatening small groups instead of the whole class (Kraft, 1985)

Category 3
apply strategies in categories 1 and 4

Figure 25. Pedagogical changes for enhancing BE students' WTC.

Rutherford and Ahlgren (1990) believe that students need to practice what they learned over and over again in order to fully master the acquired knowledge and then be confident to use it.

（2）While high WTC students have supportive classroom contexts，teachers should remain be helpful to BE students in the second category.

（3）In contrast to the first category，if the contextual factors are supportive but individual students in the fourth category are unwilling to communicate，English teachers of BE students ought to help them find new ways of learning. Students need to initiate communication and stay active in English classrooms；a major problem given the cultural contexts identified earlier. Hence, instructors need to develop techniques that encourage students to develop positive self-perception and accommodate students to socially supportive environments (Paulsen, Bru & Murberg, 2006). For example, BE students can experience evaluation in less-threatening small groups instead of the whole class (Kraft, 1985). Effective learning requires not only structuring the links between new concepts and old ones, but also sometimes rebuilding learners' thoughts (Rutherford & Ahlgren, 1990). In this sense, students should be encouraged to develop new ideas to enrich their knowledge system. Considering owning WTC as one effective way of learning, students are able to develop their knowledge system in language speaking skills in the communication process.

(4) In circumstances students lack both WTC and contextual factors, strategies in the first and third points should be drawn by teachers to help students in the third category to increase WTC.

A challenge here is that these expected strategies are suggested in other countries rather than China where embeds different cultural values. It is mentioned that Chinese learners of English tend to be other-directed and follow the submissive way of learning due to the collective Chinese culture (Wen & Clément, 2003). It is likely that they are more sensitive to judgments from others upon their language behaviors in English classes, and thus be less willing to speak in English. But along with the process of globalization, the stereotyped view of the collectivistic outlook of the Chinese is challenged (Garrott, 1995; Shi, 2006).

10.3   Limitations and future research

This investigation on Chinese BE students' willingness to communicate in English language classrooms in a university of China has its limitations. The two raters had some disagreements concerning the assessments of task difficulty. Thus, more rigorously designed classroom observations with more explicit assessment criteria can be considered in future. Also, it is conducted only with BE students, but other contexts, such as of non-BE students may be different. But rigidly managed studies are recommended to focus on small contexts at the individual level to probe "the content of learning and the relationship between students, teachers, and institutions" (Benson & Voller, 1997). Gao (2005) also claims the importance of paying attention to the sub-groups and sub-values of individual learners, instead of simply assuming that Chinese learners in different places, such as North America, can be grouped into the same category under the label of Chinese culture. Thus while making use of the pedagogical implications in this case study to other contexts for Chinese L2 learners, English classroom teachers should have resilient use of these suggestions and reflect on what is suitable for their students.

This study built on the history of L2 WTC research and conducted in the Chinese BE student context. If needed, future research can be conducted to study other Chinese learners of English in classroom contexts by teachers in other situation-specific contexts, then compare with the outcomes with those found in this thesis while suggesting pedagogical strategies to enhance their students' WTC. Moreover, since quantitative and qualitative study results showed some differences, future research can be conducted to probe more about BE students' anxiety, DC, group cohesiveness and affiliation through a longitudinal study.

10. 4   Conclusion

This case study indicated that various interrelated personal and contextual factors influenced Chinese BE students' WTC in spoken English in English classrooms. BE students as a whole were somewhat willing to communicate, of moderate level. Some factors impeded their WTC, such as problems raised in teacher support in the societal context factors, risk-taking and tolerance of ambiguity in the personality factor, as well as inhibited monitor and positive expectation of evaluation in the attitudes factors. Other factors were found to be inconsistent in quantitative and qualitative data analysis. That is, low anxiety, which linked with task-orientation in the motivation factor benefited students' WTC in self-reported questionnaires while it blocked students' WTC in interviews. Also, group cohesiveness in the societal context factor and affiliation in the motivation factor were found to facilitate BE students' WTC whereas questionnaire outcomes suggested these two aspects at the moderate level can be better improved. Thus, findings in the whole thesis are partially in line with the grounded theory of Wen and Clément's (2003) Chinese conceptualization of WTC, in which Chinese learners of English with universal DC in classrooms have to overcome hindrances of the four factors in order to achieve the general WTC. English teachers in the future can apply the pedagogical strategies suggested in this book to the Chinese learners of English in China or even around the world for developing their English spoken skills and removing the stereotyped view of silent English related to Chinese learners.

References

Adamson, B. (2002). Barbarian as a foreign language: English in China's schools. *World Englishes*, 21(2), 231—43.

Adamson, B. (2004). *China's English. A history of English in Chinese education*. Hong Kong: Hong Kong University Press.

Adendorff, R. (1996). The functions of code switching among high school teachers and students in KwaZulu and implications for teacher education. In K. Bailey & D. Nunan (eds.), *Voices from the language classroom: Qualitative research in second language education* (pp. 388—406). Cambridge, England: Cambridge University Press.

Alexander, R. (2000). *Culture & pedagogy: International comparisons in primary education*. USA, UK, Australia: Blackwell Publishing.

Allison, P. D. (2003). Missing data techniques for structural equation modeling. *Journal of Abnormal Psychology*, 112 (4), 545—557.

Alwin, D. E. (1997). Feeling thermometers versus 7-point scale: Which are better? *Sociological Methods & Research*, 25(3), 318—340.

Ames, C. (1992). Achievement goals and the classroom motivational climate. In D. H. Schunk & J. L. Meece

(eds.), *Student perceptions in the classroom* (pp. 327—348).
Hillsdale, NJ: Erlbaum.

Apollo. (2009). An answer to how many normal universities are in China. Retrieved March 10, 2011, from: http://wenwen. soso. com/z/q150689640. htm.

Argyle, M. &. Dean, J. (1965). Eye-contact, distance and affiliation. *Sociometry*, 28(3), 289—304.

Bandalos, D. L. &. Finney, S. J. (2010). Factor analysis: Exploratory and confirmatory. In G. R. Hancock &. R. O. Mueller (eds.), *The reviewer's guide to quantitative methods in the social sciences* (pp. 93—114). New York: Routledge.

Bautista, M. L. S. (1997). *English is an Asian language.* Sydney, Australia: The Macquarie Library.

Bell, F. L. (2005). Comprehension aids, Internet technologies and the reading of authentic materials by adult second language learners (Ph. D. dissertation, The Florida State University).

Bell, J. (1999). *Doing your research project: A guide for first-time researchers in education and social science* (3rd ed.). Buckingham, Philadelphia: Open University Press.

Bell, R. T. (1981). *An introduction to applied linguistics: Approaches, and methods in language teaching.* London: Batsford.

Ben-Gal, I. (2005). Outlier detection. In O. Maimon &. L. Rokach (eds.), *The data mining and knowledge discovery handbook* (pp. 131—142). Israel: Springer.

Benson, P. &. Voller, P. (1997). Introduction. In P. Benson &. P. Voller (eds.), *Autonomy and independence in language learning* (pp. 1—17). London, New York: Longman.

Bentler, P. M. (1990). Comparative fit indexes in structural models. *Psychological Bulletin*, 107, 238—246.

Bertrand, M. & Mullainathan, S. (2001). Do people mean what they say? Implications for subjective survey data. *The American Economic Review*, 91(2), 67—72.

Bolton, K. (2003). *Chinese Englishes: A sociolinguistic history*. Cambridge: Cambridge University Press.

Bond, M. H. & Hwang, K. K. (1986). The social psychology of Chinese people. In M. H. Bond (ed.), *The psychology of Chinese people* (pp. 213—266). Oxford: Oxford University Press.

Bowen, G. A. (2009). Document analysis as a qualitative research method. *Qualitative Research Journal*, 9(2), 27—40.

Braine, D. (1999). *Non-native educators in English language teaching*. Mahwah, NJ: Lawrence Erlbaum.

Bronfenbrenner, U. (1995). Developmental ecology through space and time: A future perspective. In P. Moen, G. H. Elder, Jr. & K. Luscher (eds.), *Examining lives in context: Perspectives on the ecology of human development* (pp. 619—647). Washington, DC: American Psychological Association.

Brown, G. T. L. (2004). Measuring attitude with positively packed self-report ratings: Comparison of agreement and frequency scales. *Psychological Reports*, 94(3,Pt1), 1015—1024.

Brown, L. (2008). Language and anxiety: An ethnographic study of international postgraduate students. *Evaluation and Research in Education*, 21(2), 75—95.

Burgoon, J. K. (1976). Coping with communication anxiety and reticence in the classroom. *Florida Speech Communication Journal*, 4, 13—21.

Buss, A. R. & Royce, J. R. (1975). Detecting cross-cultural commonalties and differences: Intergroup factor analysis. *Psychological Bulletin*, 82, 128—136.

Byrne, B. M. (2010). *Structural equation modeling with AMOS: Basic concepts, applications and programming* (2nd ed.). New York: Routledge.

Cao, Y. Q. (2011). Investigating situational willingness to communicate within second language classrooms from an ecological perspective. *System*, 39, 468—479.

Cao, Y. & Philp, J. (2006). Interactional context and willingness to communicate: A comparison of behavior in whole class, group and dyadic interaction. *System*, 34(4), 480—493.

Cetinkaya, Y. B. (2005). Turkish college students' willingness to communicate in English as a foreign language. PhD Dissertation. Columbus: The Ohio State University.

Cheng, L. Y. (2008). The key to success: English language testing in China. *Language Testing*, 25(1), 15—37.

Cheung, G. W. & Rensvold, R. B. (2002). Evaluating goodness-of-fit indexes for testing measurement invariance. *Structural Equation Modeling*, 9, 233—255.

China University Alumni Association (2010). The reveal of the year 2010 ranking list of China's universities, introducing the starred ranking of China's universities for the first time. Retrieved November 8, 2010, from: http://www.cuaa.net/cur/2010.

China Education Newspaper (2011). 2011 name list of eligible colleges and universities for student enrollment. Retrieved April 16, 2012, from: http://edu. people. com. cn/GB/116076/14598457. html.

Clandinin, D. J. &. Connelly, F. M. (2000). *Narrative inquiry: Experience and story in qualitative research*. San Francisco: Jossey-Bass Publishers.

Clément, R. , Dörnyei, Z. &. Noels, K. A. (1994). Motivation, self-confidence, and group cohesion in the foreign language. *Language Learning*, 3, 417—448.

Coffey, A. &. Atkinson, P. (1996). *Making sense of qualitative data: Complementary research strategies*. London: Sage.

Cohen, L. , Manion, L. , &. Morrison, K. (2000). *Research methods in education* (5th ed.). London, New York: Routledge.

Cohen, J. (1992). A Power Primer. *Psychological Bulletin*, 112(1), 155—159.

Cook, V. (2002). Language teaching methodology and the L2 user perspective. In V. Cook (ed.), *Portraits of the L2 user* (pp. 327—343). Clevedon. : Multilingual Matters.

Creswell, J. W. (2008). *Educational research: Planning, conducting, and evaluating quantitative and qualitative research* (3rd ed.). Upper Saddle River, N. J. : Prentice Hall.

Crystal, D. (1997). *English as a global language*. New York: Cambridge University Press.

Davis, S. F. &. Palladino, J. J. (2004). *Psychology*(4th ed.). Upper Saddle River, N. J. : Prentice Hall.

de Saint Léger, D. & Storch, N. (2009). Learners' perceptions and attitudes: Implications for willingness to communicate in an L2 classroom. *System*, 37(2), 269—285.

de Vaus, D. (2000). *Surveys in social research* (5th ed.). Sydney: Allen & Unwin; London: Routledge.

de Vaus, D. (2002). *Analysing social science data: 50 key problems in data analysis*. London, California, New Delhi: Sage Publications.

Denscombe, M. (2003). *The good research guide: For small-scale social research projects*. Maidenhead: Open University Press.

Deterding, D. (2006). The pronunciation of English by speakers from China. *English World-Wide*, 27(2), 175—198.

Dörnyei, Z. (2001). *Teaching and researching motivation*. New York: Longman.

Dörnyei, Z. (2003). Attitudes, orientations, and motivations in language learning: Advances in theory, research, and applications. *Language Learning*, 53, 3—32.

Dörnyei, Z. (2007). *Research methods in applied linguistics: Quantitative, qualitative, and mixed methodologies*. Oxford University Press, Oxford.

Edwards, J. G. H. (2007). Teaching pronunciation in twenty-first century China: Models and methods. In J. Liu (ed.) *English language teaching in China: New approaches, perspectives and standards* (pp. 270—284). London, New York: Continuum.

Ely, C. M. (1986). Language learning motivation: A descriptive and causal analysis. *The Modern Language Journal*, 70(1), 28—35.

Enders, C. K. & Peugh, J, L. (2004). Using an EM covariance matrix to estimate structural equation models with missing data: Choosing an adjusted sample size to improve the accuracy of inferences. *Structural Equation Modeling*, 11 (1), 1—19.

ELT Advisory Board under the Ministry of Education (2000). The English teaching syllabus for Bachelor of English students in higher education. Retrieved March 15, 2011, from: http://wenku. baidu. com/view/e05b052e453610661ed9f47f. html.

Fan, C. Y. , Chen, C. F. & Lin, H. P. (1998). Helping Chinese students to develop sensitivity to English rhythm. *Studies in English Language and Literature*, 3, 13—17.

Fan, X. & Sivo, S. A. (2007). Sensitivity of fit indices to model misspecification and model types. *Multivariate Behavioral Research*, 42(3), 509—529.

Ferguson, G. (2006). *Language planning and education*. Edinburgh: Edinburgh University Press.

Fontana, A. , & Frey, J. H. (1994). Interviewing: the art of science. In N. K. Denzin & Y. S. Lincoln (eds.) *Collecting and interpreting qualitative materials* (pp. 361—367). Thousand Oaks, Calif. : Sage Publications.

Ford, J. K. , Schmitt, N. , Schechtman, S. L. , Hults, B. M. & Doherty, M. L. (1989). Process tracing methods: contributions, problems, and neglected research questions. *Organisational Behaviour and Human Decision Processes*, 43, 75—117.

Fraenkel, J. R. & Wallen, N. E. (2006). *How to design and evaluate research in education* (6th ed.). Boston, Mass. : McGraw-Hill.

Freeman, D. & Freeman, Y. (2004). *Essential linguistics : What you need to know to teach reading, ESL, spelling, phonics, grammar.* Portsmouth, NH : Heinemann.

Fushino, K. (2010). Causal relationships between communication confidence, beliefs about group work, and willingness to communicate in foreign language group work. *TESOL Quarterly*, 44(4), 700—724.

Gan, Z. D. (2011). Second language task difficulty : Reflections on the current psycholinguistic models. *Theory and Practice in Language Studies*, 1(8), 921—927.

Gao, Y. (2000). Email to Z. Xu [Online], 17 Nov. , Available : Email : xuz@spectrum. curtin. edu. au [17 November 2000].

Gao, X. (2005). A tale of two mainland Chinese English learners. *Asian EFL Journal*, 7(2), 1—20.

Gardner, R. C. (1985). *Social psychology and second language learning : The role of attitudes and motivation.* London : Edward Arnold.

Gardner, R. C. (2000). Correlation, causation, motivation, and second language acquisition. *Canadian Psychology/ Psychologiecanadienne*, 41(1), 10—24.

Garrott, J. R. (1995) Chinese cultural values : New angles, added insights. *International Journal of Intercultural Relations*, 19(2), 211—225.

Garver, M. S. & Mentzer, J. T. (1999). Logistics research methods : Employing structural equation modeling to test for construct validity. *Journal of Business Logistics*, 20 (1), 33—57.

Ge, X. R. & Gao, Y. Y. (2005). An investigation into teachers' and learners' perceptions of the corrective feedback.

Journal of Western Chongqing University (*Social Sciences Edition*), 4(4), 70—80.

Geng, J. X. (2007). Removal of toxic English teaching & learning styles in China. *US-China Education Review*, 4(5), pp. 42—45.

Graddol, D. (2006). *English next*. London: The British Council.

Gregersen, T. & Horwitz, E. K. (2002). Language learning and perfectionism: Anxious and non-anxious language learners' reactions to their own oral performance. *The Modern Language Journal*, 86(4), 562—570.

Guariento, W. & Morley, J. (2001). Text and task authenticity in the EFL classroom. *ELT Journal*, 55 (4), 347—353.

Guo, T. (2007). A case study of teacher's codeswitching behaviors in mainland China's university EFL classrooms and students' reactions to the codeswitching. Doctoral dissertation. Oxford: University of Oxford.

Halliday, M. A. K. (1990). *Spoken and Written Language*. Oxford: Oxford University Press.

Hamm, J. V., Farmer, T. W., Dadisman, K., Gravelle, M. & Murray, A. R. (2011). Teachers' attunement to students' peer group affiliations as a source of improved student experiences of the school social-affective context following the middle school transition. *Journal of Applied Developmental Psychology*, 32, 267—277.

Hammersley, M. (1992). Deconstructing the qualitative-quantitative divide. In J. Brannen (ed.), *Mixing methods: Qualitative and quantitative research* (pp. 39—55).

Aldershot: Avebury Ashgate Publishing.

Harris, L. R. & Brown, T. L. G. (2010). Mixing interview and questionnaire methods: Practical problems in aligning data. *Practical Assessment, Research & Evaluation*, 15 (1), 1—19.

Harte, J. M., Westenberge, R. M., & Van Someren, M. (1994). Process models in decision making. *Acta Psychologica*, 87, 95—120.

Hill, M. (1997). SPSS Missing Value Analysis 7.5. Chicago: SPSS.

Ho, L. (2003). Pronunciation problems of PRC students. In L. G. Ling, L. Ho, J. E. L. Meyer, C. Varaprasad & C. Yong (eds.) *Teaching English to students from China* (pp. 138—157). Singapore: Singapore University Press.

Hoe, S. L. (2008). Issues and procedures in adopting structural equation modeling technique. *Journal of Applied Quantitative Methods*, 3(1), 76—83.

Hoelter, D. R. (1983). The analysis of covariance structures: Goodness-of-fit indices. *Sociological Methods and Research*, 11, 325—344.

Hooper, D., Coughlan, J. & Mullen, M. R. (2008). Structural equation modelling: Guidelines for determining model fit. *Electronic Journal of Business Research Methods*, 6(1), 53—60.

Horwitz, E. K. (2000). Horwitz comments: It ain't over 'til it's over: On foreign language anxiety, first language deficits, and the confounding of variables. *The Modern Language Journal*, 84(2), 256—259.

Horwitz, E. K. (2008). *Becoming a language teacher: A*

practical guide to second language learning and teaching. Boston: Pearson Education.

Hu, G. W. (2002). Potential cultural resistance to pedagogical imports: The case of communicative language teaching in China. *Language, Culture and Curriculum*, 15(2), 93—105.

Hu, X. Q. (2004). Why China English should stand alongside British, American and the other "World Englishes". *English Today*, 20(2), 26—33.

Hu, X. Q. (2005). China English, at home and in the world. *English Today*, 21(3), 27—38.

Huang, Z. C. & Pan, J. P. (2011). The factor analysis on the "dumb English" education problem in China, Japan and Korea. *Studies in Foreign Education*, 38(8), 5—8.

Hyland, F. (2003). Focusing on form: Student engagement with teacher feedback. *System*, 31, 217—230.

Irvine, S. H. (1969). Contributions of ability and attainment testing in Africa to a general theory of intellect. *Journal of Biosocial Science*, 1, 91—102.

Jagacinski, C. M. (1992). The effects of task involvement and ego involvement on achievement-related cognitions and behaviors. In D. H. Schunk & J. L. Meece (eds.), *Student perceptions in the classroom* (pp. 307—326). Hillsdale, NJ: Erlbaum.

Jenkins, J. (2006). Current perspectives on teaching World Englishes and English as a lingua franca. *TESOL Quarterly*, 40(1), 157—81.

Jia, G. J. & Xiang, M. Y. (1997). Wei zhongguoyingyuyibian (In defense of China English). *Waiyuyuwaiyujiaoxue*

(*Foreign Languages and Foreign Languages teaching*), 101
(5), 11—12.

Jin, J. (2005). Which is better in China, a local or a native
English-speaking teacher? *English Today*, 21(3), 39—46.

Jin, L. & Cortazzi, M. (2003). English language teaching in
China: A bridge to the future. In W. Ho and R. Wong
(eds.), *English language teaching in East Asia today:
Changing policies and practices* (pp. 131—46). Singapore:
Eastern Universities Press.

Johnson, R. B. & Onwuegbuzie, A. J. (2004). Mixed methods
research: A research paradigm whose time has come.
Educational Researcher, 33(7), 14—26.

Jöreskog, K. & Sörbom, D. (1993). *LISREL* 8: *Structural
equation modeling with the SIMPLIS command language.*
Chicago, IL: Scientific Software International Inc.

Jørgensen, J. N. (2005). Plurilingual conversations among
bilingual adolescents. *Journal of Pragmatics*, 37(3), 391—
402.

Kachru, B. B. (1992). *The other tongue: English across
cultures*(2nd ed.). Urbana: University of Illinois Press.

Kang, S. (2005). Dynamic emergence of situational willingness
to communicate in a second language. *System*, 33(2), 277—
292.

Kaya, M. (1995). The relationship of motivation, anxiety, self-
confidence, and extroversion/introversion to students' active
class participation in an EFL classroom in Turkey.
Unpublished Master Thesis. Ankara: Bilkent University.

Kearney, P., Plax, T. G., Richmond, V. P., & McCroskey,
J. C. (1984). Power in the classroom IV: Alternatives to

discipline. In R. N. Bostrom (ed.), *Communication Yearbook 8* (pp. 724—746). Beverly Hills, CA: Sage.

Kerlinger, F. N. (1970). *Foundations of behavioral research*. New York: Holt, Rinehart and Winston.

Kirkpatrick, A. (1999). English as an Asian language: Implications for the English language curriculum. In 4SEA Conference, Singapore [22—24 November].

Kirkpatrick, A. (2006). Which model of English: Native-speaker, Nativised or lingua franca? In M. Saraceni & R. Rubdy (eds.), *English in the world: Global rules, global roles* (pp. 71—83). London, New York: Continuum.

Kirkpatrick, A. (2007). *World Englishes: Implications for international communication and English language teaching*. Cambridge: Cambridge University Press.

Kirkpatrick, A. & Xu, Z. C. (2002). Chinese pragmatic norms and China English. *World Englishes*, 21(2), 269—80.

Kraft, R. G. (1985). Group-inquiry turns passive students active. *College Teaching*, 33(4), 149—154.

Kuhl, J. (1994). Action vs. state orientation: Psychometric properties of the Action Control Scale (ACS—90). In J. Kuhl & J. Beckmann (eds.), *Volition and personality* (pp. 47—59). Gottingen: Hogrefe & Huber Publishers.

Kvale, S. (1996). *Interviews: An introduction to qualitative research interviewing*. Thousand Oaks, Ca.: Sage Publications.

Labov, W. (1972). *Language in the inner city: Studies in the Black English vernacular*. Philadelphia: University of Pennsylvania Press.

Lakin, J. C. & Chartrand, T. L. (2003). Using nonconscious

behavioral mimicry to create affiliation and rapport. *Psychological Science*, 14(4), 334—339.

Lapadat, J. C. (2000). Problematizing transcription: Purpose, paradigm and quality. *International Journal of Social Research Methodology*, 3, 203—219.

Leary, M. R. (1983). A brief version of the Fear of Negative Evaluation Scale. *Personality and Social Psychology Bulletin*, 9, 371—376.

Levine, G. S. (2003). Student and instructor beliefs and attitudes about target language use, first language use, and anxiety: Report of a questionnaire study. *The Modern Language Journal*, 87(3), 343—364.

Li, D. C. S. (2007). Researching and teaching China and Hong Kong English. *English Today*, 23(3&4), 11—17.

Li, W. Z. (1993). Zhongguoyingyuyuzhongguoshiyingyu (China English and Chinese English). *WaiyuJiaoxueyuyanjiu (Foreign Languages Teaching and Researching)*, 96(4), 18—24.

Liebscher, G. & Dailey-O'Cain, J. (2005). Learner code-switching in the content-based foreign language classroom. *The Modern Language Journal*, 89(2), 234—247.

Liu, J. (1999). Nonnative-English-speaking professionals in TESOL. *TESOL Quarterly*, 33(1), 85—102.

Liu, M. (2006). Anxiety in Chinese EFL students at different proficiency levels. *System*, 34, 301—316.

Liu, M. (2007). Chinese students' motivation to learn English at the tertiary level. *Asian EFL Journal*, 9(1), 126—146.

Liu, M. & Jackson, J. (2008). An exploration of Chinese EFL learners' unwillingness to communicate and foreign language anxiety. *The Modern Language Journal*, 92(1), 71—86.

Liu, S. L. & Li, P. (2005). Formative evaluation analysis in college English teaching. *Education and Vacation*, 35, 118—119.

Liu, X. F., Chang, Q. & Gan, C. (2010). On the influence of learning attitudes on 90s-born college students' English learning. *Education for Chinese After-school*, 16, 38.

Liu, Z. D. (2012). Wenzhou university. Retrieved May 22, 2012, from: http://baike. baidu. com/view/54133. htm.

Long, M. (1996). The role of the linguistic environment in second language acquisition. In W. C. Ritchie & T. K. Bhatia (eds.), *Handbook of second language acquisition* (pp. 413—468). New York: Academic Press.

Lyle, J. (2003). Stimulated recall: A report on its use in naturalistic research. *British Education Research Journal*, 29 (6), 861—878.

Ma, Y. N., Zhang, L. X. & Hu, S. J. (2004). Current situation analysis and solutions on students' learning attitudes in higher education in Zhejiang Province. *Journal of Hangzhou Institute of Electronic Engineering*, 25(4), 49—51.

Macaro, E. (2001). Analysing student teachers' codeswitching in foreign language classrooms: Theories and decision making. *The Modern Language Journal*, 85(4), 531—548.

MacIntyre, P. D. (1992). Anxiety, language learning and stages of processing. Unpublished doctoral dissertation. London, Canada: University of Western Ontario.

MacIntyre, P. D. (1994). Variables underlying willingness to communicate: A casual analysis. *Communication Research*

Reports, 11, 135—142.

MacIntyre, P. D. (1995a). How does anxiety affect second language learning? A reply to Sparks and Ganschow. *Modern Language Journal*, 79, 90—99.

MacIntyre, P. D. (1995b). On seeing the forest and the trees: A rejoinder to Sparks and Ganschow. *Modern Language Journal*, 79, 245—247.

MacIntyre, P. D. (2007). Willingness to communicate in the second language: Understanding the decision to speak as a volitional process. *The Modern Language Journal*, 91(4), 564—576.

MacIntyre, P. D., Babin, P. A. & Clément, R. (1999). Willingness to communicate: Antecedents and consequences. *Communication Quarterly*, 47, 215—229.

MacIntyre, P. D., Baker, S. C., Clément, R. & Conrod, S. (2001). Willingness to communicate, social support and language learning orientations of immersion students. *Studies in Second Language Acquisition*, 23, 369—388.

MacIntyre, P. D., Baker, S., Clément, R. & Donovan, L. (2002). Sex and age effects on willingness to communicate, anxiety, perceived competence, and L2 motivation among junior high school French immersion students. *Language Learning*, 52, 537—564.

MacIntyre, P. D., Burns, C. & Jessome, A. (2011). Ambivalence about communicating in a second language: A qualitative study of French immersion students' willingness to communicate. *The Modern Language Journal*, 95(1), 81—96.

MacIntyre, P. D., Dörnyei, Z., Clément, R., & Noels, K.

(1998). Conceptualizing willingness to communicate in a L2: A situational model of L2 confidence and affiliation. *The Modern Language Journal*, 82(4), 545—562.

MacIntyre, P. D. & Doucette, J. (2010). Willingness to communicate and action control. *System*, 38, 161—171.

MacIntyre, P. D. & Gardner, R. C. (1989). Anxiety and second-language learning: Toward a theoretical clarification. *Language Learning*, 39, 251—275.

MacIntyre, P. D. & Legatto, J. J. (2011). A dynamic system approach to willingness to communicate: Developing an idiodynamic method to capture rapidly changing affect. *Applied Linguistics*, 32(2), 149—171.

Matsubara, K. (2007). Classroom group dynamics and motivation in the EFL context. In K. Bradford-Watts (ed.), *JALT 2006 Conference Proceedings* (pp. 209—220). Tokyo: JALT.

Matsuoka, R. & Evans, D. R. (2005). Willingness to communicate in a second language. *J Nurs Studies N C N J*, 4(1), 3—12.

Matthews, G. & Deary, I. J. (1998). *Personality traits*. Cambridge: Cambridge University Press.

McArthur, T. (2002). *The Oxford guide to world Englishes*. Oxford: Oxford University Press.

McCroskey, J. C. (1992). *An introduction to communication in the classroom*. Edina, Minnesota: Burgess International Group.

McCroskey, J. C. (1997). *An introduction to communication in the classroom* (7th ed.). Edina, Minnesota: Burgess International Group.

McCroskey, J. C., Andersen, J. F., Richmond, V. P. & Wheeless, L. R. (1981). Communication apprehension of elementary and secondary students and teachers. *Communication Education*, 30, 122—132.

McCroskey, J. C., & Baer, J. E. (1985, November). Willingness to communicate: The construct and its measurement. Paper presented at the annual convention of the *Speech Communication Association*, Denver, CO.

McCroskey, J. C., Fayer, J. & Richmond, V. P. (1985). Don't speak to me in English: Communication apprehension in Puerto Rico. *Communication Quarterly*, 33, 185—192.

McCroskey, J. C. & Richmond, V. P. (1987). Willingness to communicate and interpersonal communication. Morgantow, WV: West Virginia Symposium on Personality and Interpersonal Communication.

McCroskey, J. C. & Richmond, V. P. (1989). Bipolar scales. In P. Emmert & L. L. Baker (eds.), *Measurement of communication behavior* (pp. 154—167). New York: Longman.

McCrosky, J. C. & Richmond, V. P. (1990). Willingness to communicate: A cognitive view. *Journal of Social Behavior and Personality*, 5, 19—37.

McDonald, R. P. & Ho, M. H. R. (2002). Principles and practice in reporting structural equation models. *Psychological Methods*, 7, 64—82.

McGroarty, M. (1998). Constructive and constructivist challenges for applied linguistics. *Language Learning*, 48, 591—622.

McKay, S. L. (2002). *Teaching English as an international*

language. Oxford: Oxford University Press.

McKay, S. (2003). Toward an appropriate EIL pedagogy: Re-examining common ELT assumptions. *International Journal of Applied Linguistics*, 13(1), 1—22.

McKay, S. L. (2006). EIL curriculum development. In M. Saraceni & R. Rubdy (eds.), *English in the world: Global rules, global roles* (pp. 114—129). London, New York: Continuum.

McQuitty, S. (2004). Statistical power and structural equation models in business research. *Journal of Business Research*, 57(2), 175—183.

Medgyes, P. (1994). *The non-native teacher*. London: Macmillan.

Meredith, W. (1993). Measurement invariance, factor analysis and factorial invariance. *Psychometrika*, 58, 525—543.

Mills, A., Wiebe, E. & Durepos, G. (2010). *Encyclopedia of case study research*. Thousand Oaks, CA: Sage.

Millsap, R. E. & Everson, H. (1991). Confirmatory measurement model comparisons using latent means. *Multivariate Behavioral Research*, 26, 479—497.

Millsap, R. E. & Hartog, S. B. (1988). Alpha, beta, and gamma changes in evaluation research: Astructural equation approach. *Journal of Applied Psychology*, 73, 574—584.

Mishan, F. (2005). *Designing authenticity into language learning materials*. Bristol: Intellect.

Mortensen, C. D., Arntson, P. H. & Lustig, M. (1977). The measurement of verbal predispositions: Scale development and application. *Human Communication Research*, 3(2), 146—158.

Norton, B. & Toohey, K. (2001) Changing perspectives on good language learners. *TESOL Quarterly*, 35(2), 307—322.

Nunan, D. (2001). *Second language teaching and learning*. Beijing: Foreign Language Teaching and Research Press.

Oguz, A. & Bahar, H. O. (2008). The importance of using authentic materials in prospective foreign language teacher training. *Pakistan Journal of Social Sciences*, 5(4), 328—336.

Patton, M. Q. (2002). *Qualitative evaluation and research methods* (3rd ed.). CA, London, New Delhi: Sage.

Paulsel, M. L. (2004). Effective instructional practice. Using behavior alternation techniques to mange student behavior. *Communication Teacher*, 18(2), 44—48.

Paulsen, E., Bru, E. & Murberg, T. A. (2006). Passive students in junior high school: the associations with shyness, perceived competence and social support. *Social Psychology of Education*, 9(1), 67—81.

Peng, J. E. (2007). Willingness to communicate in the Chinese EFL classroom: A cultural perspective. In J. Liu (ed.), *English language teaching in China: New approaches, perspectives, and standards* (pp. 250—269). London: Continuum.

Peng, J. E. (2008). An empirical study on university students' willingness to communicate in English from a cultural perspective. *Language Teaching and Linguistic Studies*, 6, 30—36.

Peng, J. E. (2012). Towards an ecological understanding of willingness to communicate in EFL classrooms in China.

System, 40, 203—213.

Peng, J. E. &. Woodrow, L. (2010). Willingness to communicate in English: A model in the Chinese EFL classroom context. *Language Learning*, 60(4), 834—876.

Peterson, E. R., Brown, G. T. L. &. Irving, S. E. (2010). Secondary school students' conceptions of learning and their relationship to achievement. *Learning and Individual Differences*, 20, 167—176.

Phillipson, R. (1992). *Linguistic imperialism*. Oxford: Oxford University Press.

Pichette, F. (2009). Second language anxiety and distance language learning. *Foreign Language Annals*, 42(1), 77—93.

Poland, B. D. (1995). Transcription quality as an aspect of rigor in qualitative research. *Qualitative Inquiry*, 1, 290—310.

Poland, B. D. (2001). Transcription quality. In J. F. Gubrium &. J. A. Holstein (eds.), *Handbook of interview research : Context and method* (pp. 629—649). Thousand Oaks, CA: Sage.

Punch, K. (1998). *Introduction to research methods in education*. Thousand Oaks, CA: Sage, 149—282.

Qing, N. &. Wolff, M. (2003). The Chinglish syndrome: Do recent developments endanger the language policy of China? *English Today*, 19(4), 30—35.

Richard-Amato, P. A. (2003). *Making it happen : From interactive to participatory language teaching : Theory and practice*. White Plains, NY: Pearson Education.

Richards, J. C. (2006). *Communicative language teaching today*. New York: Cambridge University Press.

Richmond, V. P. & Roach, K. D. (1992). Willingness to communicate and employee success in US organizations. *Journal of Applied Communication Research* , 20, 95—115.

Riordan, C. M. & Vandenberg, R. J. (1994). A central question in cross-cultural research : Do employees of different cultures interpret work-related measures in an equivalent manner? *Journal of Management* ,20, 643—671.

Rolin-Ianziti, J. & Brownlie, S. (2002). Teacher use of learners' native language in the foreign language classroom. *Canadian Modern Language Review* , 58(3), 402—426.

Rooney, P. (2005). Researching from the inside—does it compromise validity? A discussion. *Level 3* , 3.

Rutherford, F. J. & Ahlgren, A. (1990). *Science for all Americans*. New York : Oxford University Press.

Rymes, B. (2009). *Classroom discourse analysis : A tool for critical reflection*. Cresskill, NJ : Hampton Press.

Sallinen-Kuparinen, A. , McCroskey, J. C. & Richmond, V. P. (1991). Willingness to communicate, communication apprehension, introversion, and self-reported communication competence : Finnish and American comparisons. Jyvaskyla, Finland : World Communication Association Convention.

Sandelowski, M. (2000). Focus on research methods : Combining qualitative and quantitative sampling, data collection and analysis techniques in mixed-method studies. *Research in Nursing & Health* , 23, 246—255.

Savignon, S. J. (2005). Communicative language teaching : Strategies and goals. In Hinkel, E. (ed.), *Handbook of research in second language teaching and learning* (pp. 635—652). Mahwah, NJ : Lawrence Erlbaum.

Savignon, S. J. (2007). Beyond communicative language teaching: What's ahead? *Journal of Pragmatics*, 39, 207—220

Scarcella, R. C. & Oxford, R. L. (1992). *The tapestry of language learning: The individual in the communicative classroom.* Boston: Heinle.

Schiller. H. I. (1976). *Communication and cultural domination.* White Plains, N. Y. : Sharpe.

Schmidt, R. & Watanabe, Y. (2001). Motivation, strategy use, and pedagogical preferences in foreign language learning. In Z. Dörnyei & R. Schimidt (eds.), *Motivation and second language acquisition* (pp. 311—357). Honolulu: University of Hawai'i, Second language Teaching and Curriculum Center.

Schreiber, J. B. , Nora, A. , Stage, F. K. , Barlow, E. A. & King, J. (2006). Reporting Structural Equation Modeling and Confirmatory Factor Analysis Results: A Review. *The Journal of Educational Research* , 99(6), 323—337.

Schunk, D. H. (1996). Goal and self-evaluative influences during children's cognitive skill learning. *American Education Research Journal*, 33(2), 359—382.

Shi, L. J. (2006). The successors to Confucianism or a new generation? A questionnaire study on Chinese students' culture of learning English. *Language, Culture and Curriculum*, 19(1), 122—147.

Shrum, J. L. & Glisan, E. W. (2000). *Teacher's handbook: Contextualized language instruction.* Boston: Heinle & Heinle.

Sijtsma, K. (2009). On the use, the misuse, and the very

limited usefulness of Cronbach's alpha. *Psychometrika*, 74 (1), 107—120. doi: 10. 1007/S11336-008-9101-0.

Simic, M. & Tanaka, T. (2008). Language context in the willingness to communicate research works: A review. *Journal of Humanities and Social Sciences*, 26, 71—88.

Sivo, S. A., Fan, X., Witta, E. L. &Willse, J. (2006). The search for "optimal" cutoff properties: Fit index criteria in structural equation modeling. *Journal of Experimental Education*, 74(3), 267—288.

Skinner, E. A. & Belmont, M. J. (1993). Motivation in the classroom: Reciprocal effects of teacher behavior and student engagement across the school year. *Journal of Educational Psychology*, 85, 571—581.

Smith, A. N. (1971). The importance of attitude in foreign language learning. *The Modern Language Journal*, 55(2), 82—88.

Smith, C. P. (2000). Content analysis and narrative analysis. In H. T. Reis & C. M. Judd (eds.), *Handbook of Research Methods in Social and Personality Psychology* (pp. 313—335). Cambridge: Cambridge University Press.

Someren, M., Barnard, Y. V. & Sandberg, J. (1994). *The think aloud method*. London: Academic Press.

Sparks, R., Ganschow, L. & Javorsky, J. (2000). Déjà vu all over again: A response to Saito, Horwitz, and Garza. *Modern Language Journal*, 84, 251—255.

Spielberger, C. (1966). The effects of anxiety on performance in complex learning tasks. In C. Spielberger (ed.), *Anxiety and behavior* (pp. 361—396). New York: Academic Press.

Steiger, J. H. (1989). *EzPATH: Causal modeling*. Evanston,

IL: SYSTAT.

Suzuki, S. & Rancer, A. S. (1994). Argumentativeness and verbal aggressiveness: Testing for conceptual and measurement equivalence across cultures. *Communication Monographs*, 6, 256—279.

Swain, M. (1985). Communicative competence: Some roles of comprehensible input and comprehensible output in its development. In S. Gass & C. Madden (eds.), *Input in second language acquisition* (pp. 235—252). Rowley, MA: Newbury House.

Swain, M. (1995). Three functions of output in second language learning. In G. Cook & B. Seidlhofer (eds.), *Principles and practice in the study of language: Studies in honour of H. G. Widdowson* (pp. 125—144). Oxford: Oxford University Press.

Swain, M. (2000). The Output Hypothesis and beyond. In J. P. Lantolf (ed.), *Sociocultural theory and second language learning* (pp. 97—114). Oxford: Oxford University Press.

Tabachnick, B. G. & Fidell, L. S. (2007). *Using multivariate statistics* (5th ed.). New York: Allyn and Bacon.

Tashakkori, A. & Teddlie, C. (1998). *Mixed methodology: Combining qualitative and quantitative approaches.* Thousand Oaks, CA: Sage.

Terry, D. J., Hogg, M. A. & Duck, J. M. (1999). Group membership, social identity and attitudes. In D. Abrams & M. A. Hogg (eds.), *Social identity and social cognition* (pp. 280—314). Oxford: Blackwell.

Timina, S. A. & Butler, N. L. (2011). Uncomfortable topics and their appropriateness in Asian EFL classes. Retrieved

December 23, 2011, from: http://www. uobabylon. edu. iq/uobColeges/ad_downloads/5_31560_1069. pdf.

Trimpop, R. M. (1994). *The psychology of risk-taking behavior*. North-Holland: Elsevier Science B. V.

Tuckman, B. W. (1972). *Conducting educational research*. New York: Harcourt Brace Jovanovich, Inc.

Twenty-first Century. (2007). Ministry of Education approved the establishment of Business English programme. Retrieved March 10, 2011, from: http://elt. i21st. cn/article/1406_1. html.

van der Meij, H. & Zhao, X. G. (2010). Codeswitching in English courses in Chinese universities. *The Modern Language Journal*, 94(3), 396—411.

Wang, R. P. (1994). *Shuo dong dao xi huayingyu (Talking about English)*. Beijing: Waiyujiaoxueyuyanjiuchubanshe (Foreign Language Teaching and Researching Press).

Wang, Y. H. (2010). Connotation, features, types and design of English classroom tasks. *Journal of Basic English Education*, 12(4), 10—17.

Warden, C. A. & Lin, H. J. (2000). Existence of integrative motivation in an Asian EFL setting. *Foreign Language Annals*, 33(5), 535—545.

Wei, Y. & Fei, J. (2003). Using English in China. *English Today*, 19(4), 42—7.

Wen, W. & Clément, R. (2003). A Chinese conceptualisation of willingness to communicate in ESL. *Language, Culture and Curriculum*, 16(1), 18—38.

Wheaton, B. , Muthen, B. , Alwin, D. F. & Summers, G. (1977). Assessing reliability and stability in panel models.

Sociological Methodology, 8(1), 84—136.

White, R. V. (1988). *The ELT curriculum: Design, innovation and management*. Oxford, Cambridge: Blackwell Publishers.

Witcher, C. S. G. (2010). Negotiating transcription as a relative insider: Implications for rigor. *International Journal of Qualitative Methods*, 9(2), 122—132.

Wu, D. X. (2008). An investigation of Chinese EFL learners' self-perceived communicative competence and willingness to communicate. *Modern Foreign Languages*, 31(3), 280—290.

Wu, M. L. (2009). *Structural equation modeling-AMOS computation and application*. Chongqing: Chongqing University Press.

Wu, Z. & Wen, W. (2009). Undergraduate BE students' willingness to communicate in L2: The effects of societal context, motivational orientation, personality factors and affective perceptions. *Foreign Language Teaching and Practices*, 1, 32—56.

Wuensch, K. (2010). Karl Wuensch's Statistics Lessons. Retrieved December 23, 2011, from: http://core. ecu. edu/ psyc/wuenschk/statslessons. htm.

Wuhan University (2008). The publication of the first national investigation of "1990s-generation" freshmen. *China Youth Daily*, December 11, 2008.

Xie, Z. J. (1995). Zhongguoyingyu: Kuawenhuayuyanjiaojizhong de ganraoxingbianti (China English: An interference variety in cross-cultural communication). *Xiandaiwaiyu (Modern languages)*, 70

(4), 7—11.

Xu, Z. C. (2002). From TEFL to TEIL: Changes in perceptions and practices: Teaching English as an international language (EIL) in Chinese universities in P. R. China. In A. Kirkpatrick (ed.), *English in Asia: Communication, identity, power & education* (pp. 225—244). Melbourne: Language Australia Ltd.

Xu, Z. (2005). Chinese English. What is it and is it to become a regional variety of English? PhD Dissertation, Curtin University of Technology, Perth, Australia.

Xu, Z. C. (2002). From TEFL to TEIL: Changes in perceptions and practices: Teaching English as an international language (EIL) in Chinese universities in P. R. China. In A. Kirkpatrick (ed.) *English in Asia: Communication, identity, power & education* (pp. 225—244). Australia: Language Australia Ltd.

Yardley, L. & Bishop, F. (2008). Mixing qualitative and quantitative methods: a pragmatic approach. In C. Willig & W. Stainton-Rogers (eds.) *The SAGE handbook of qualitative research in psychology* (pp. 352—371). Los Angeles, London, New Delhi, Washington DC: Sage.

Yashima, T. (2002). Willingness to communicate in a second language: The Japanese EFL context. *The Modern Language Journal*, 86(1), 54—66.

Yashima, T., Zenuk-Nishide, L. & Shimizu, K. (2004). Influence of attitudes and affect on willingness to communicate and L2 communication. *Language Learning*, 54, 119—152.

Yin, R. K. (1994). *Case study research: Design and methods*

(2nd ed.). Thousand Oaks, CA: Sage.

Yin, R. K. (2006). Case study methods. In J. L. Green, G. Gamilic, P. B. Elmore, A. Skukauskaité & E. Grace (eds.), *Handbook of complementary research methods in education research* (pp. 111—122). Mahwah, N. J.: Lawrence Erlbaum Associates; Washington, D. C. : American Educational Research Association.

Yin, R. K. (2009). *Case study research : Design and methods* (4th ed.). Los Angeles, CA: Sage Publications.

Yu, D. H. (1990). The hidden stories of the Chinese. *Chinese Psychology Series 3* (pp. 1—14). Taipei: Professor Zhang Press, Inc.

Yu, D. H. & Gu, B. L. (1990). Chinese face concerns. *Chinese Psychology Series 3* (pp. 63—107). Taipei: Professor Zhang Press, Inc.

Yu, M. (2011). Effect of communication variables, affective variables, and teacher immediacy on willingness to communicate of foreign language teachers. *Chinese Journal of Communication*, 4(2), 218—236.

Yu, J. (2010). A survey on different anxiety level students' attitudes towards teachers' corrective feedback in the classrooms. *Forum on Contemporary Education*, 1, 13—14.

Zhang, H. (2011). Language anxiety in ESL classroom: Anxiety of turn-taking patterns in ESL classroom discourse. *2011 International Conference on Education, Research and Innovation*, 18, Singapore: IACSIT.

Zhang, L. J. (2006). The ecology of communicative language teaching: Reflecting on the Singapore experience. *The Annual CELEA International Conference : Innovating*

English Teaching: Communicative Language Teaching (CLT) and Other Approaches. China: CELEA and Guangdong University of Foreign Studies, Guangzhou.

Zhang, Y. , Gan, Y. & Cham, H. (2007). Perfectionism, academic burnout and engagement among Chinese college students: A structural equation modeling analysis. *Personality and Individual Differences*, 43, 1529—1540.

Zhao, Y. & Campbell, K. P. (1995). English in China. *World Englishes*, 14(3), 377—90.

Zhao, Y. P. (2009). 'Silent English' phenomenon and English learning. *The Science Education Article Collects*, 1, 154—155.

Zheng, Y. (2008). Anxiety and second/foreign language learning revisited. *Canadian Journal for New Scholars in Education*, 1(1), 1—12.

Appendix A
WTC Questionnaires in Spoken English in English Language Classrooms

Please write down your personal information. All the information you provide in the questionnaires will be confidential.

Name: _____/ Student number: _____

Gender: ☐Male ☐Female

Grade: ☐1 ☐2 ☐3 ☐4

Major: ☐English Education ☐Business English

(1) WTC inside the classroom

Directions: This questionnaire is composed of statements concerning your feelings about communication with other people while speaking in class in English. Imagine you are faced with the following situations that would require you to use English. How willing do you feel to use English in each situation?

a) For BEE students：

	1	2	3	4	5	6
	Strongly unwilling	*Mostly unwilling*	*slightly willing*	*moderately willing*	*mostly willing*	*strongly willing*
1. Talk with foreigners about your daily life in English.						
2. Make a speech on a familiar topic in English.						
3. Read an English article loud and clear in the class.						
4. Talk with native English speakers in English in class.						
5. Read a poem with clear tones and rhymes in English.						
6. Talk with your teacher in English.						
7. Retell a story in English.						
8. Do a role play in English.						
9. Discuss a topic with your peers in English.						

Continued

	1	2	3	4	5	6
	Strongly unwilling	*Mostly unwilling*	*slightly willing*	*moderately willing*	*mostly willing*	*strongly willing*
10. Debate with your peers in English.						

b) For BBE students

	1	2	3	4	5	6
	Strongly unwilling	*Mostly unwilling*	*slightly willing*	*moderately willing*	*mostly willing*	*strongly willing*
1. Have a job interview in English.						
2. Pick up a phone call in English.						
3. Make a speech in English.						
4. Present in a conference in English.						
5. Greet someone in English.						
6. Organize a meeting in English.						

Continued

	1	2	3	4	5	6
7. Work with your partners in English.						
8. Do an oral English translation.						
9. Negotiate a business affaire in English.						
10. Talk with an unhappy client in English.						

(2) Personality

Directions: Please use this list of common human traits to describe yourself as accurately as possible. Describe yourself as you see yourself at the present time, not as you wish to be in the future. Describe yourself as you are generally or typically, as compared with other persons you know of the same sex and of roughly your same age. Please circle one number that applies to you for each pair of adjectives.

Ex.

Emotional 1 2 3 4 5 6 7 8 9 Unemotional

If you think you are emotional, circle 1. If you think you are unemotional, circle 9. If you think your being emotional or unemotional is not absolute but happens in degrees, choose the number that represent you best.

Silent	1 2 3 4 5 6 7 8 9	Talkative
Timid	1 2 3 4 5 6 7 8 9	Bold
Inactive	1 2 3 4 5 6 7 8 9	Active
Inhibited	1 2 3 4 5 6 7 8 9	Spontaneous
Unassertive	1 2 3 4 5 6 7 8 9	Assertive
Unadventurous	1 2 3 4 5 6 7 8 9	Adventurous

Revised from Cetinkaya (2005)

（3） DC （items 17-20） &-Affiliation （items 21-25） (Matsubara, 2007) &-Positive Expectation of Evaluation (items 26-31) (Revised from Leary (1983))

Directions: This questionnaire is composed of statements concerning your feelings about English learning in classrooms. To what extent do you agree or disagree with these statements?

	1	2	3	4	5	6
	very strongly disagree	*mostly disagree*	*slightly agree*	*moderately agree*	*mostly agree*	*very strongly agree*
17. When I have assignments to do in English, I try to do them immediately.						
18. I try to read English newspapers or magazines outside my English course work.						
19. I would like the number of English classes at school increased.						

Continued

	1	2	3	4	5	6
	very strongly disagree	*mostly disagree*	*slightly agree*	*moderately agree*	*mostly agree*	*very strongly agree*
20. I find myself studying English more than other students.						
21. It is effective to study as a group, which is composed of people who fit together.						
22. I enjoy studying with a group, which is composed of people who fit together.						
23. I want to remain a member of a group, which I have worked together previously.						
24. I come to like the members of a group while interacting with that particular group.						
25. There was a feeling of unity and cohesion when working as a group which was composed of people who fit together.						
26. I worry about what other people will think of me even when I know it doesn't make any difference.						

Continued

	1	2	3	4	5	6
	very strongly disagree	*mostly disagree*	*slightly agree*	*moderately agree*	*mostly agree*	*very strongly agree*
27. I am frequently afraid of other people noticing my shortcomings.						
28. I am afraid others will not approve of me.						
29. I am afraid that people will find fault with me.						
30. I am usually worried about what kind of impression I make.						
31. I often worry that I will say or do the wrong things.						

(4) Anxiety

Directions: Below are six situations in which you might need to communicate. Please indicate how nervous you are to communicate in each of the situations described below. Indicate in the space provided at the left of each item your estimate of your anxiety.

Presume 0 = completely relaxed and 100 = extremely nervous.

_____ 32. Have a small-group conversation in English with acquaintances.

_____ 33. Talk in English in a large meeting among friends.

_____ 34. Talk in English to friends.

_____ 35. Talk in English to acquaintances.

_____ 36. Give a presentation in English to a group of acquaintances.

_____ 37. Talk in English to a small group of friends.

Revised from MacIntyre and Doucette (2010)

(5) Perceived communication competence

Directions: Below are six situations in which you might need to communicate. Please indicate how competent you are to communicate in each of the situations described below. Indicate in the space provided at the left of each item your estimate of your competence.

Presume 0＝completely incompetent and 100＝competent.

_____ 38. Have a small-group conversation in English with acquaintances.

_____ 39. Give a presentation in English to a group of friends.

_____ 40. Have a small-group conversation in English with strangers.

_____ 41. Talk in English in a large meeting among friends.

_____ 42. Talk in English in a large meeting with acquaintances.

_____ 43. Give a presentation in English to a group of acquaintances.

Revised from Cetinkaya (2005)

Thank you for your cooperation!

Appendix B
Classroom Observation Sheet

Degree of WTC: □High □Low

duration of an classroom interaction (total 45 minutes)	type of an interaction						how hard a task is (rang from 1= extremely easy to 6 = extremely hard)	WTC (rang from 1= strongly unwilling to 6 = strongly willing)
	T-S		S-S					
	T-C	T-G	T-I	I-C	I-G	I-I		

Note: T= teacher, S= student(s), C= class, G= group of students, I= individual student.

Appendix C
Stimulated Recall Questions

After videotaping each class, ask the participant following questions:

1. Did you like this task? Why? Why not?

2. How useful for your learning do you think this task was? Why? Why not?

3. Did you think you did this task well? Why? Why not?

4. Did you enjoy doing this task? Why? Why not?

5. Did you feel happy to work in this group/pair? What did you feel happy/not happy with?

6. Comparing the two tasks you did, which task did you prefer? Why? Which group did you prefer? Why?

Adapted from Cao and Philp (2006)

Appendix D
Interview Questions with BE Students

General questions (for first visit before conducting the first interview): Ask for personal information, such as names; inquire about general views of spoken English in English language classrooms as follows:

1. How important it is for you to learn English?

2. How good are you at learning English? What do you think your English level is? Especially in spoken English?

3. Do you like speaking in English classrooms?

4. Please describe your willingness to communicate in English classrooms.

Opening declaration: briefly mention the purpose of the study to participants.

Open-ended interview questions include four aspects:

Societal Context (group cohesiveness & teacher support)

1. What do you think about the idea of hanging with some of your classmates as a group in the class (e. g. sit with them or talk with them)? If yes, how do feel about communicating with them in classrooms? If no, please state your reasons.

2. How do you feel about communicating with other students in the class?

3. How do you feel about the size of your classroom? In

267

your opinion how large is the appropriate classroom size?

4. How much time do you spend with your teachers in a week? In what situations?

5. What are your teachers' attitudes towards students? How close do you think you are with your teachers?

6. How do you feel about your teachers' communications with students in the class?

Personality Factors (risk-taking & tolerance of ambiguity)

7. Can you describe your personality (quiet or talkative, relaxed or tense)?

8. What do you think about asking questions in the class?

9. How do you feel about volunteering an answer in the class?

10. When a linguistic point puzzles you, what will you do?

11. When you are unsure about a speaking topic, what will you do?

Motivational Orientation (affiliation & task orientation)

12. With whom do you feel most comfortable to communicate?

13. How do you feel about doing a speaking task in the class?

14. What will you do to see the meaning of the task?

15. How do you assess your speaking abilities, on your own referenced standards or on public recognition?

Affective Perceptions (inhibited monitor & positive expectation of evaluation)

16. How do you feel about seeking final answers from grammar to situations in English?

17. What do you think about other students' speaking

abilities?

18. How do you feel when your teacher asks you to answer a question?

19. What do you pay attention to when you are speaking English in the class?

20. Who do you think stimulate or decrease your motivation to communicate with others in the class?

Appendix E
Interview Questions with English Teachers

1. Can you please describe your experience of learning English as a student before?

2. How do you teach in the English language class? Why?

3. How do you think about your students' communication with you in the class? Why?

4. How do you think about students' communication with each other in the class? Why?

5. What will you do, if your students can not do what you want them to do in oral English?

6. What suggestions would you provide for future improvement?

Appendix F
Thematic Coding of Qualitative Data

		High WTC		Low WTC	
		Personal	Contextual	Personal	Contextual
Societal context	Group cohesiveness				
	Teacher support				
Personality factors	Risk-taking				
	Tolerance of ambiguity				
Motivational orientation	Affiliation				
	Task-orientation				
Affective perceptions	Inhibited monitor				
	Positive expectation of evaluation				

271

Appendix G
A Sample Student Narrative

Opening declaration: please write one past and one present spoken English learning experience in lessons. It is required to include interactions among teachers and you and classmates in past and present English lessons, your perceptions towards the interactions, WTC in speaking English and reasons of your high or low WTC.

The sample narrative was from:

Number	Student name	Programme (Year)	Sex	WTC	Present classroom context
S10	Zhou	BBE (2)	male	low	weak

The original narrative (in simplified Chinese):

高中那会学习英语,其实我都是抱着很大热情的。可能是自己对英语感兴趣吧。记得那时候上英语课,老师会让我们跟读新单词。这之后会进入课文文章。老师通常会让我们听课文的音频。然后我们就跟着音频通读全文。这其中,我们要理解文章大概意思,划出疑点、难点,以及不懂的单词、词组等。重点是找出每一段的中心句。我挺喜欢这种方式的。一方面可以弄懂单词的发音,另一方面可以培养我的阅读能力。接着就是老师讲加上学生回答的环节了。学生回答一般分为三种。第一种就是自己举手回答了。记得那时我也会举手回答一下。第二种就是老师点名回答了。这点的话就是知道答案的话还好,不知道的话就比较郁闷了。第三种就是以横排或纵排为单位来回答,这个还蛮有意思的。记得那时读单词的强烈热情,至今仍觉得不可思议。

上了大学,我明显感觉到自己对学习英语的热情下降了。可能是学习方式改变了,又或许是老师的上课方式不适合自己的。第二个学期,由于要应付专四考试和专四口语考试,大家的学习任务更重了。每节课的任务就是做练习。虽然有点枯燥,但由于考试当头,同学们还是有理智并认真对待每一次练习。毕竟,高中的英语学习侧重基础。而大学里的发散思维则要求同学们,尤其是作为英语专业同学的我们,对英语学习有更大的深度和广度。另外,我个人不太喜欢做选择题。而更喜欢对外国的文化、文学之类的接触。

Translation:

While learning English in high school, actually I was full of enthusiasm, because I was interested in learning English. I remember when having English lessons at that time, the teacher first asked us to follow her to read new words. Then we went on to study the text. The teacher usually let us listened to the audio of the text. Then we read the whole text after the audio. Through reading, we should understand the general idea of the text; and underline confusing language points and difficult points as well as some unfamiliar words and phrases and so on. One important thing was to find out the topic sentence of each paragraph. I really liked this way of learning. On one hand, I could figure out words' pronunciations. On the other hand, this way of learning improved my reading skills. In the next section, the teacher asked students to answer questions about the text. There were three ways of student answering. The first way was a student raised one's hand to answer questions. I remembered at that time I sometimes raised my hands. The second way was the teacher nominated someone to answer. As to this way, if I knew the answer, it would be fine. If I did not know the answer, it would be quite gloomy. The third way was to answer in a row or in a column. This was quite interesting. Until now, I still feel amazing about the strong enthusiasm that I had while reading words.

After entering the university, I clearly feel that my enthusiasm falls sharply. This may because the way of learning changed or may because the teacher's way of teaching is not suitable for me. In this second semester, because we have to pass TEM4 and TEM4 speaking test, our learning tasks are heavier. Every lesson's task is to do exercises. Though it is somewhat boring, the tests are coming and all classmates are sober-minded and treat every exercise seriously. After all, English learning in high school emphasized basic knowledge learning. But in university, divergent thinking is required for students. Especially as Bachelor of English students, we need to learn English in more depth and width. Personally, I don't like to do multiple choices of A, B, C, and D. I prefer the learning of foreign culture and literatures.